OXFORD THINKERS

Class Book 4

Sarah Phillips

OXFORD

Syllabus

		Vocabulary	Grammar	Cross-curricular topic, Culture and Values	Literacy
S **Starter**	**What's fun about *The Big Question?*** Page 4	High numbers 1,000–1,000,000	*Why / Because* *Why are you a member of The Big Question?* *Because I learn new things on it.* *Before / After* *When do you use The Big Question?* *Before / After I finish my homework.*		
1	**What can we do in different seasons?** Page 8	Outdoor summer activities Winter activities	*Wh-* questions with *did* *Where did he go?* *will / won't* *I think I'll go skiing.* *We won't win the challenge.*	**Science:** learning about life cycles **Culture:** a traditional Native North American festival **Values:** expressing feelings and ideas through poems	**Reading:** a poem **Writing (AB Pages 14–15):** The Big Write: a Big Question post about seasonal activities **Tip:** exclamation marks
2	**What's great about a zoo?** Page 20	Zoo animals Zoo keeper jobs	*going to* affirmative, negative and questions *They're going to film tigers.* *have to* affirmative and negative *He has to clean the cages.*	**Art:** learning about camouflage **Culture:** Mountain chicken frogs **Values:** protecting animals	**Reading:** a zoo information panel **Writing (AB Pages 24–25):** The Big Write: a Big Question post about going to the zoo **Tip:** using paragraphs
3	**What's fun about an after-school club?** Page 32	Types of films Clothes	Present continuous vs present simple *What are you watching?* *What do you usually watch?* **Expressions of frequency** *How often … ?* *Once / twice / three times a week.* *Every week.*	**Music:** tempo, pitch and volume **Culture:** end-of-year party in the USA **Values:** taking part in a community event	**Reading:** emails **Writing (AB Pages 34–35):** The Big Write: a Big Question post about a popular club **Tip:** using *or*
Extensive Reading 1 Page 44		Book reviews: *Black Beauty*			
The Big Project 1 Page 46		Draw a giant animal. **English in use:** *Shall I … ? Shall I colour the squares?*			
4	**What's exciting about exploring?** Page 50	Geographical features Birds	Present perfect third person singular affirmative and negative *She's trekked across a desert.* *She hasn't walked on the moon.* **as … as** *It's as colourful as a parrot.*	**History:** the exploration of Saturn **Culture:** visiting Angel Falls **Values:** taking interest in your surroundings	**Reading:** a diary **Writing (AB Pages 48–49):** The Big Write: a Big Question post about exploring **Tip:** gerunds
5	**How can we help at home?** Page 62	Indoor chores Outdoor chores	Present perfect questions and short answers *Have you made your bed?* *Yes, I have. / No, I haven't.* **Present perfect affirmative and negative** *I've watered the plants.* *I haven't cut the grass.*	**Maths:** using a pie and bar chart **Culture:** helping at home in India **Values:** thinking before you act	**Reading:** a folk tale **Writing (AB Pages 58–59):** The Big Write: a Big Question post about helping at home **Tip:** *it's* or *its*

What's fun about *The Big Question*?

Lesson 1 Review and song

1 **Think** 💭 **Look at the photos and answer.**

1 How do the children know each other?   **2** What can they do on *The Big Question* website?

2 **Listen to the song and check your ideas.** 🔊 001

Ben

Mason

Our website's name is The Big Question.
The website gives us a Big Question.
There are lots of answers to the Big Question,
And we share our answers here.

1 Ben shared a photo of a camping holiday.
2 Noah had a chat about computer games.
3 Ania sent a post about some ducks on the sea.
4 Sophie sent a song about a day on the beach.
5 Tess shared a photo of her town in the past.
6 Lily sent a song about heroes in her class.
7 Dev played a video game, he climbed a wall.
8 Mason played an instrument, the Trumptar Drumbal.
Chorus

Noah

Dev

Ania

Sophie

Tess

Lily

3 **Match the song lines with the pictures.** 📝 **Then sing.** 🔊 001

a  **b**  **c**  **d**

e   **f**   **g**   **h**

S Lesson 2 Review and grammar

1 **Think** 💭 What was your favourite lesson in *Oxford Thinkers* 3?

2 Look at the avatars and at the photos of the children. What are the avatars' names?

3 Read and match the answers to the questions. 📘

The Big Question survey result!

Why do our members like *The Big Question* website?
Here are your answers to these three questions.

1 Why are you a member of *The Big Question*?

2 When do you use *The Big Question*?

3 What do you like best about *The Big Question*?

a I like its video game best. It's fun!

b After I finish my homework.

c Before I go to bed.

d Because I can chat with my friends on it.

e Because I learn new things on it.

f Because I think the answers to the Big Questions are interesting.

g After school.

h I like its avatars best. They're cool.

4 Look, listen and read. 🔊 002

Why is Tess a member of *The Big Question*?

Because she can chat with her friends on it.

5 **Communicate** 💬 Ask and answer with *Why* and *Because*.

watch videos

chat with friends

read about different countries

make friends

listen to songs

share photos

1 Listen, point and repeat. 🔊 004

2 Listen and point. 🔊 005

1,000	**5,000**
10,000	**25,000**
30,000	**100,000**
150,000	**500,000**
575,000	**1,000,000**

3 Listen, point and repeat. 🔊 006

1 plus   **2** minus   **3** equals

4 times   **5** divided by

4 Say the sums. Match with the answers.

one million   two hundred and fifty thousand
four hundred thousand   fifteen thousand

1 **5,000 + 10,000 =**
2 **500,000 − 100,000 =**
3 **1,000,000 ÷ 4 =**
4 **250,000 × 4 =**

5 BEFORE YOU READ The children guess the number of marbles in a tank in this story. How many marbles do you think there are?

THE BiG Quest — Maths World

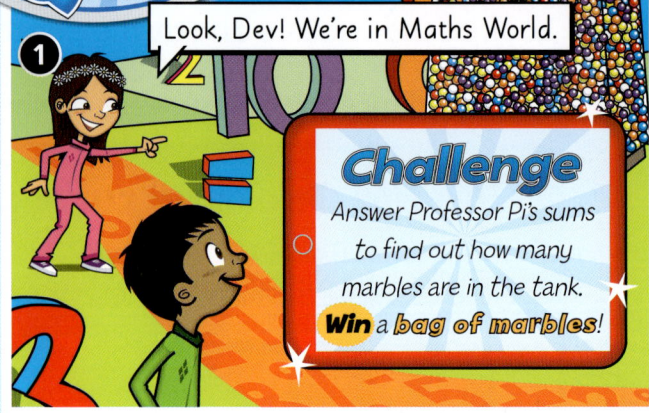

1 Look, Dev! We're in Maths World.

Challenge
Answer Professor Pi's sums to find out how many marbles are in the tank. **Win** a *bag of marbles!*

2 Wow! There are thousands!

Shh! Here's Professor Pi with his first sum.

Hello! There are 4,800 purple marbles. And there are 200 more orange marbles than purple marbles.

3 OK. 4,800 + 200 = 5,000. So, there are 5,000 orange marbles!

🟠 5,000

6 Listen, read and check your ideas. 🔊 007

7 AFTER YOU READ
Watch the story video. ▶
Complete the activities. AB Pages 4–5

4 Good! Now listen. There are three times more white marbles than orange marbles.

$5,000 \times 3 = 15,000$. Easy! There are 15,000 white marbles.

15,000

5 I love maths! Can you give us the sum for the blue marbles, please, Professor Pi?

6 There are four times more purple marbles than blue marbles.

Let me think. 4,800 purple marbles, but fewer blue marbles! Hmm … I know! $4,800 \div 4 = 1,200$ blue marbles!

1,200

7 Here's my next sum. There are 1,500 fewer yellow marbles than orange marbles.

My turn! There are 5,000 orange marbles. So $5,000 - 1,500 = 3,500$ yellow marbles!

3,500

8 Now, the red marbles! Hey! Where are the red marbles?

Wait a minute. Here's Lucky with a clue!

Find Trick! His favourite colour is red!

9 Look over there! Trick has got all the red marbles.

Give us the marbles, Trick!

10 498.

499.

500.

Now let's add up all the numbers!

500

11

$$
\begin{array}{r}
4,800 \\
5,000 \\
15,000 \\
1,200 \\
3,500 \\
500\ + \\
\hline
30,000
\end{array}
$$

The answer is 30,000.

Correct! Well done!

Come on! Let's have a game of marbles.

LEVEL UP >>>

1 What can we do in different seasons?

Ellie's star post ⭐

We can make apple pies in autumn.

Sing along with Ania

Look with Mason

Winter World

Find out with Ben

Discover with Tadi

BIG POLL
Which season do you prefer?
spring summer
autumn winter

THE BIG QUESTION

1 Look and answer.

1 What's the Big Question for unit 1?
2 Who are the posts from?
3 What can you see in the pictures?

2 Which things do you see in the Big Question video? Watch then say. ▷

- an apple pie
- a table
- a TV
- a forest
- potatoes
- carrots
- eggs
- green peppers
- a knife
- ice cream

3 **Think** 💭 What are your answers to the Big Question?

Keep a list of your answers on the Big Question poster.

> **UNIT 1** | **THE BIG QUESTION POSTER**
> What can we do in different seasons?
>
> **OUR ANSWERS**

4 Answer the Big Poll.

5 Watch the Big Question video again. ▷ Complete the activities. **AB Page 6**

Ania

1 **Think** 💭 What fun things can people do outdoors in summer?

2 Listen, point and repeat. 🔊 010 Compare your list with Ania's.

3 Say which activities you *often*, *sometimes* and *never* do in summer.

Ania's list

What can we do in different seasons?
We can do fun things outdoors in summer.

1 have a barbecue   **2** go horse riding   **3** pick strawberries   **4** play mini-golf   **5** go hiking

6 learn to windsurf   **7** go mountain biking   **8** do a treasure hunt   **9** go to an outdoor cinema   **10** grow a sunflower

4 **Listen and sing.** 🔊 011

Summer time is fun, fun, fun!
Summer time is great!
What did you do in the summer,
In your summer holiday?
What did you do? Did you go hiking?
Did you take a bike and go mountain biking?
What did you do in the summer,
Outdoors in the summer?

We had a barbecue in the garden.
We did a treasure hunt in the garden.
I grew a sunflower in the garden
Outdoors in the summer!

Chorus

I went horse riding with my friends.
I learned to windsurf with my friends.
I played mini-golf with my friends
Outdoors in the summer!

Chorus

I had fun, yes, I had fun.
I had fun in the summer!
I had fun, yes, I had fun.
Outdoors in the summer!

5 **Communicate** 💬 Say true and false sentences about your summer holidays. 🔊 012

I went to an outdoor cinema.   I think that's true.

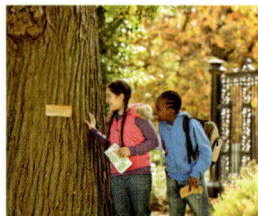

I had a treasure hunt.   I don't believe you. False!

1 Lesson 3 Grammar

1 Listen, read and look at the picture. 🔊 013

Where were Ania and her friend?

Hi! I went horse riding in the summer. Look at this photo!

I love it. Who did you go with?

I went with my friend Eve.

Where did you go?

We went round the lake. It was really nice.

What did you see?

There were some pretty flowers, and we saw some birds and a deer, too!

2 Listen and follow. 🔊 014 Ask and answer about your summer holiday.

Where			go?	I	went to the beach.
Who	did	you he	go with?	He	went with my family.
What		she	see? do?	She	saw a train. played mini-golf.

3 Look, listen and read. 🔊 015

What did he do in the summer?

He had a barbecue.

Where did he go?

He went to the park.

Who did he go with?

He went with Jake.

I know! It's Fred.

4 Communicate 💬 Play the game.

Fred

Jake

Moh

1 **Think** 💭 What can you do in winter?

2 Listen, point and repeat. 🔊 017

3 Which are indoor activities?
Which are outdoor activities?

What can we do in different seasons?   **Mason**

We can do a lot of fun things in winter.

Mason's list

1 go skiing   **2** go sledging

3 make a snowman   **4** do crafts

5 make soup   **6** make a bird feeder

THE BiG Quest   **Winter World**

① We're in Winter World. It's beautiful!

Look at the snow! I think I'll go skiing.

② **Challenge**
Make a realistic snowman.
Win a *sledge ride!*

I need your help, Lily.

③ Will you be back soon?

Yes, I will. Don't worry. Bye, Mason!

4 **BEFORE YOU READ** This is a story about making a snowman. What does a snowman usually look like?

5 Listen and read. 🔊 018 What does the snowman in the story look like?

6 **AFTER YOU READ** Watch the story video. ▷
Complete the activities. **AB Page 9**

4 1 HOUR LATER

Oh dear. My snowman isn't very good. I don't think it looks realistic. We won't win the challenge.

5 This is fun. I've got time to go down once more. Then I'll help Mason with the snowman.

6 What are you doing? Be careful! You'll hurt someone!

7 Hey! That's my leg! Oh no! I can't stand up. Ouch!

8 And now I'm going backwards! Aargh!

9 Oh no! She'll hit the tree.

10 Hello Lily! Thanks. This snowman looks great. It's very realistic.

11 Hurray! Our snowman won!

Trick won't be happy.

Too bad. This is fun.

LEVEL UP >>>

1 REMEMBER THE STORY Read. Who's speaking?

1 I think I'll go skiing.

2 Will you be back soon?

3 We won't win the challenge.

4 She'll hit the tree.

Lily

Mason

2 Look at the sentences from the story. Choose the correct sentence.

a We use *will* / *won't* + infinitive to talk about future actions.

b We use *will* / *won't* + infinitive to talk about something happening now.

3 Listen and follow. 019 Think Imagine it's snowing. Talk about your ideas for after-school activities.

I He She We	'll won't	go skiing. go sledging. make a snowman. make soup. make a bird feeder. do crafts.

Look!

We often use *will* after *I think* and *I don't think*.
I think I'll go skiing.
I don't think we'll win.
Remember! We don't say:
~~I think we won't win.~~

4 Think, pair, share! Talk about your ideas for next weekend. Then talk about your partner.

go to the beach
visit my grandparents
make a cake
have a picnic
watch a DVD
play with my friends

He thinks he'll go shopping. He won't go to the cinema.

I think I'll go shopping on Saturday. I won't go to the cinema.

1 Look. Which is the correct order of stages?

a butterfly – chrysalis – egg – caterpillar
b caterpillar – butterfly – chrysalis – egg
c egg – caterpillar – chrysalis – butterfly
d egg – butterfly – caterpillar – chrysalis

What can we do in different seasons?
We can observe butterflies in spring.

Ben

Butterflies are amazing!

There are four stages in a butterfly's life cycle. At each stage the butterfly looks different. This process is called *metamorphosis*. Metamorphosis means *changing shape*.

Stage 1
The female butterfly lays **eggs** on a leaf. They're very small.

Stage 2
Caterpillars hatch from the eggs. The caterpillars eat leaves and flowers. They grow fast.

Stage 4
The chrysalis opens and the **butterfly** comes out. It can't fly, but soon its wings can move and it flies away. It looks for its food in flowers. Females find males and the cycle starts again.

Stage 3
The caterpillar stops eating and growing. It makes a **chrysalis**. The caterpillar is safe inside the chrysalis. Now the caterpillar starts changing shape. It changes into a butterfly.

2 Look, read and listen. 🔊 021 Then answer. 📝

1 Where do butterflies lay eggs?
2 What do caterpillars eat?
3 Do caterpillars grow slowly?
4 What happens inside the chrysalis?
5 What is this change called?
6 What do butterflies do when they come out of the chrysalis?

Glossary

female   male   hatch

3 **Think, pair, share!** What other animals have different stages and forms in their life cycle?

Lesson 7 Literacy: a poem

What can we do in different seasons?

Winter is a time to sit by the fire.

Tadi

1 BEFORE YOU READ Look at the title of the poem. Do you think Native North Americans enjoyed the winter?

2 Think, pair, share! Some Native North Americans gave their children a name to represent a season. Which seasons do you think these names represent?

Young Eagle   Rain Falling   Golden Leaf
Strong Wind   Field of Flowers   Sunny Day
Snow Bird   Time of Waiting

I think Young Eagle represents spring.

Why?

Because birds hatch in spring.

3 Read and listen. 023
Which picture represents the poem? Choose a, b or c.

a   b   c

Native American Winter

Cold Walker came in the night
Throwing down his white blanket
The people sat by the fire
And told their stories.

Barbara Gorelick

4 AFTER YOU READ
Complete the activities. **AB Page 12**

Big Values!
Writing poems is a good way to show your feelings and ideas.

1 Listen to Tadi talking about the Navajo Mountain Chant festival. 🔊 025 **Answer.**

Which three things does he talk about?

| painting | eating | dancing | singing |

2 Listen again. 🔊 025 **Say *a* or *b*.**

1 How long is the Navajo Mountain Chant festival?
   a five days   **b** nine days

2 When is the festival?
   a at the end of winter   **b** at the end of spring

3 What colours do they use in the sand painting?
   a red, black, yellow, green   **b** red, black, yellow, white

4 What do the dancers carry?   **a** tree branches   **b** white flowers

5 Who goes to the festival?
   a only the Navajo people   **b** the Navajo people and a lot of visitors

3 **Think, pair, share!** What are traditional festivals in your country?

4 Complete the activities. **AB Page 13**

Lesson 9 Writing   ^The **Big Write** AB Pages 14–15

Lesson 10   **THE BIG QUESTION REVIEW**

REVIEW VIDEO

1 Watch and answer the questions on the review video. ▷

2 Look back at the unit and say the missing words.
Then compare your answers on the Big Question poster.

We can make apple pies in ⬚ .

We can observe ⬚ in spring.

We can do fun things ⬚ in summer.

Winter is a time to sit by the ⬚ .

We can do a lot of fun things in ⬚ .

I love doing different things in different ⬚ .

3 **Communicate** 💬 **Ask and answer.**

Which is your favourite answer?

'We can do a lot of fun things in winter.' I love sledging!

4 Complete the self-evaluation activities. **AB Page 15**

1 **Read and match.**

1 Where did he go?
2 What did he do?
3 What did he see?
4 Who did he go with?

a He learned to surf.
b He saw a starfish.
c He went to the beach.
d He went with his friends.

2 **Complete the sentences.**

Leila and her family last spring.

1 (go) Where _____ *did Leila go* _____ last spring?
   She _____ *went* _____ to the forest.
2 (go) Who _____ with?
   She _____ with her family.
3 (see) What _____?
   She _____ a deer.

Zak and his sister last summer.

4 (go) _____ last summer?
   He _____ to a strawberry farm.
5 (go) _____ with?
   He _____ with his sister.
6 (do / pick) _____?
   He _____ strawberries.

3 **Imagine you went somewhere interesting last week. Draw a picture and write notes.**

1 Where / go? _____
2 What / do? _____
3 What / see? _____
4 Who / go with? _____

4 **Communicate** Write questions for your partner. Ask and answer using the information from activity 3.

1 *Where did you go?* _____
2 _____
3 _____
4 _____

5 **Complete the sentences.**

1 She _'ll go_____ skiing.

2 He _____won't go_____ skiing.

3 She _____ a bird feeder.

4 He _____ sledging.

5 She _____ soup.

6 She _____ sledging.

7 He _____ a bird feeder.

8 They _____ a snowman.

6 **Write the words in order to make sentences.**

1 (watch)(they'll)(a)(DVD)(.)   _They'll watch a DVD._____

2 (shopping)(we)(go)(won't)(.)   _____

3 (sledging)(I'll)(think)(go)(don't)(I)(.)   _____

4 (think)(swimming)(we'll)(I)(go)(.)   _____

7 **Think** 💭 **Think about what you will do this weekend. Tick ✔ or cross ✗.**

This weekend, I'll ...	
do my homework.	
play basketball.	
go to the park.	
listen to music.	
watch a DVD.	

8 **Communicate** 💬 **Tell your partner about what you will / won't do this weekend.**

I'll go to the park.
I won't play basketball.

2 What's great about a zoo?

Oliver's star post ⭐

We can adopt an animal.

Sing along with Dev

Look with Lily

Zoo World

Find out with Noah

Discover with Leta

BIG POLL
Are zoos ...
a good place for animals
or
a bad place for animals?

1 Look and answer.

1 What's the Big Question for unit 2?
2 Who are the posts from?
3 What can you see in the pictures?

2 Which animals do you see in the Big Question video? Watch then say. ▷

- a snake
- an elephant
- a zebra
- a bird
- a hippo
- a giraffe
- a monkey
- a spider
- a penguin
- a crocodile

3 **Think** 💭 What are your answers to the Big Question?

Keep a list of your answers on the Big Question poster.

UNIT **2**   THE BIG QUESTION POSTER

What's great about a zoo?

OUR ANSWERS

4 Answer the Big Poll.

5 Watch the Big Question video again. ▷ Complete the activities. **AB Page 16** ▷

2 Lesson 2 Vocabulary and song

What's great about a zoo?
We can see animals from all over the world.

Dev

1 **Think** 💭 What animals can you see in a zoo?

2 Listen, point and repeat. 🔊 028 Compare your list with Dev's.

3 Say which animals you'd like to see in a zoo. Which animals aren't you interested in?

Dev's list

1 frog

2 lizard

3 tiger

4 bat

5 chimpanzee

6 rhino

7 panda

8 sea lion

9 alligator

10 kangaroo

4 Listen and sing. 🔊 029

Class 4 are on the bus.
They've got a project to do.
Class 4 are on a trip.
They're going to go to the zoo.

Class 4 are at the zoo.
What are they going to do?
They're going to learn about kangaroos
And film the hippos in their pool.

Class 4 are at the zoo.
What are they going to see?
Some frogs in a pond, bats in a tree,
Pandas, rhinos and African bees.

Class 4 are at the zoo.
Where are they going to go?
They're going to go to the sea lion show
And then to the rhinos' watering hole.

Class 4 are on the bus.
Now their project is done.
They're going to go back to school.
Their trip was a lot of fun! (x2)

5 **Communicate** 💬 Ask and answer about animals in your country. 🔊 030

Do pandas live in England?

No, they don't.

Do frogs live in England?

Yes, they do.

1 **Listen, read and look at the picture.** 🔊 031

What is Dev's sister's school project about?

Hi! Look at my sister's photo. She and her class are on a school trip today.

Great! Where are they going to go?

They're going to go to the new safari park.

Oh dear. It's raining. They aren't going to see a lot of animals this afternoon.

It doesn't matter. Rain is perfect!

Why? What are they going to do?

They're going to learn about frogs. Frogs love the rain!

2 **Listen and follow.** 🔊 032 **Say true sentences about Dev's sister and her friends.**

Where				go?
	are	they	going to	
What				do?

	're		go to	the safari park. the zoo.
They		going to	learn about	frogs. tigers. lizards.
	aren't		draw	sea lions. alligators.
			film	

3 **Look, listen and read.** 🔊 033

Where are they going to go?

They're going to go to the zoo.

What are they going to do?

They're going to film tigers.

I know. It's picture A.

4 Communicate 💬 **Play the game.**

1 Think 💭 What does a zoo keeper do?

2 Listen, point and repeat. 🔊 035

3 Which jobs would you like to do?
Which wouldn't you like to do?

What's great about a zoo?

Zoo keepers have an interesting job.

Lily

Lily's list

1 clean the cages

2 help the vet

3 look after the hippos

4 observe the meerkats

5 wash the elephants

6 feed the bears

4 **BEFORE YOU READ** This is a story about a zoo. Can you guess what animals are in the story?

5 Listen, read and check your ideas. 🔊 036

6 **AFTER YOU READ** Watch the story video. ▷
Complete the activities. **AB Page 19**

THE BiG Quest — Zoo World

4 We have to help the zoo keeper. But how?

Hey. There's Lucky with a clue. A banana?

5 You pick up the key …

I'll give the elephant the banana.

Elephant House

… and open the door!

Thank you!

6 Oh no! It's late. Can you help me with the animals?

Chimpanzees
Pandas

Of course. Umm … Do you have to look after the tigers?

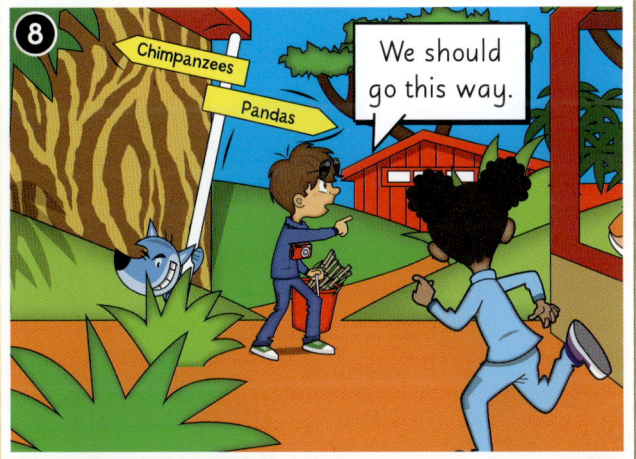

7 No, I don't. But I have to feed the pandas. Can you do that for me?

Pandas

No problem!

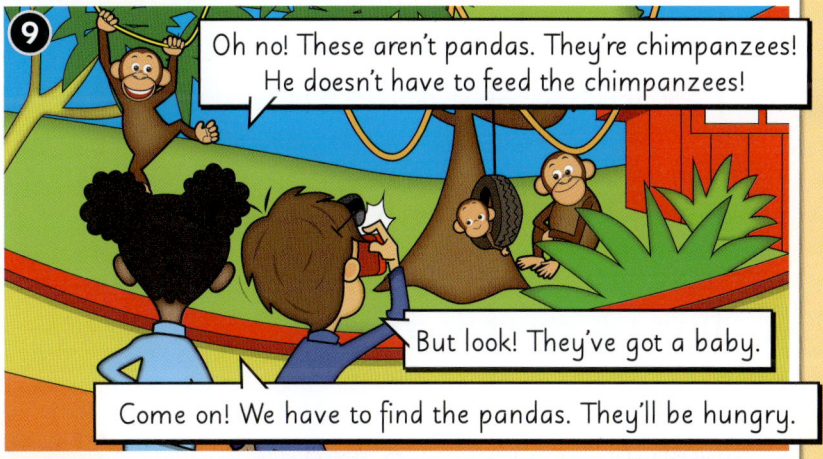

8 Chimpanzees
Pandas

We should go this way.

9 Oh no! These aren't pandas. They're chimpanzees! He doesn't have to feed the chimpanzees!

But look! They've got a baby.

Come on! We have to find the pandas. They'll be hungry.

10 Here you are, pandas!

And there's a baby. It's so cute.

We've got three photos now. Yay!

11 Wow! This is fun!

No, I don't want a fish. Thank you!

LEVEL UP ›››

1 **REMEMBER THE STORY** Read and match.

1 We have to
2 Do you have to
3 I have to
4 He doesn't have to

a feed the pandas.
b feed the chimpanzees.
c look after the tigers?
d help the zoo keeper.

Lily   Ben

2 **Look and choose.**

The zoo keeper says, 'I **have to** feed the pandas,' because …

a it's part of his job.
b he likes feeding the pandas.

> # Look!
>
> We can use *should* to make suggestions.
> *We should ask the zoo keeper.*
> *We should go this way.*

3 **Listen and follow.** 🔊 037   **Think** 💭 **Make true sentences about a lion keeper.**

I	have to	clean the cages.
He She	has to	look after the hippos. feed the bears. help the vet. wash the elephants. observe the meerkats.

I	don't		clean the cages.
He She	doesn't	have to	look after the hippos. feed the bears. help the vet. wash the elephants. observe the meerkats.

4 **Think, pair, share!** Talk about the things you have to do at home. Then talk about your partner.

feed the hamster
clean the rabbit's cage
do my homework
help my mum
make my lunch
wash my sports clothes

She doesn't have to make her lunch. She has to feed the hamster.

I have to feed the hamster. I don't have to make my lunch.

What's great about a zoo?
We can learn about animals.

Noah

1 Look at the photo. What animal can you see? Is it easy to see?

2 Read. Why do some animals need camouflage?

Some animals are difficult to see because of the colours and patterns on their bodies. This is called **camouflage** and the photo demonstrates it. Camouflage helps animals hide from other animals.

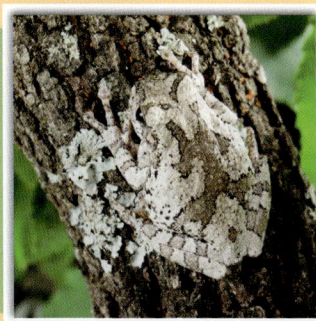

Glossary

hide   pattern

3 Read and match the instructions to the pictures.

a Draw the same patterns on the animal. Then use the same colours to colour the patterns.
b Cut out your animal. Put it on the patterns on your card. Is it easy or difficult to see?
c Draw some patterns on your card with a pencil.
d Draw an animal shape on a different piece of card. You can draw a snake, a fish or an insect.
e Now put it on your partner's patterns. Is it easy or difficult to see now? Why?
f Colour the patterns. You can use two or three colours, or you can use a lot of colours.

Find out about camouflage.
You need a pencil, a rubber, white card, scissors and wax crayons.

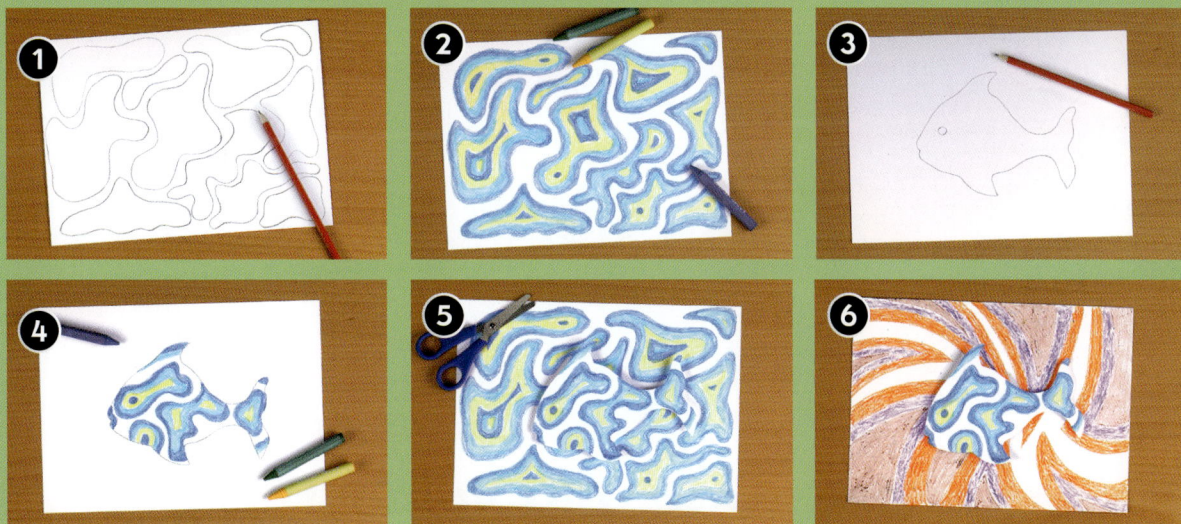

4 **Think, pair, share!** What other animals use camouflage?

Leta

1 **BEFORE YOU READ** Look at the pictures on the panel. What information can you find about black rhinos?

2 Think 💭 Why is it important for zoos to have baby animals?

3 Read and listen. 🔊 040 Were your ideas on the panel?

What's great about a zoo?
Zoos help animals in danger.

A big welcome to our new baby black rhino, Tau!

ZOO

Tau was born last month. He weighs 40 kg now. He hasn't got any horns at the moment. They're starting to grow.

WORLD RHINO DAY: 22ND SEPTEMBER

1.8 m · 1,000 kg · 1.8 m · 1,000 kg

Black rhinos are huge. They're brown, grey or white. They aren't black! They've got two horns. They're the only animals with horns on their nose. They can't see very well, but they've got a good sense of smell and hearing.

Black rhinos live in the south of Africa, in the savannah, in woods or near rivers. They eat in the morning and evening. At midday, when it's hot, they like to lie in water or mud.

Status

Every baby rhino is important, because rhinos are in danger of extinction. 200 years ago there were about 1,000,000 rhinos in Africa. Now there are less than 5,000. Sadly, baby rhinos often die in the wild. Baby rhinos born in zoos are safe. Every baby means a better future for black rhinos.

Food

fruits · flowers · leaves · roots

Big Values!
We must help and protect all animals.

4 **AFTER YOU READ**
Complete the activities. **AB Page 22**

1 Listen to Leta and her cousin Oria. 🔊 041 Answer.

What is this frog called?

2 Listen again. 🔊 041 Say *a*, *b* or *c*.

1 How much does a mountain chicken weigh?
   a more than 1 kg   **b** 2 kg   **c** 3.5 kg

2 Why is it called a mountain chicken?
   a It can fly.   **b** It's got feathers.   **c** It tastes like chicken.

3 How many mountain chickens are there in the wild?
   a about 15   **b** about 25   **c** about 50

4 What do mountain chickens eat?   **a** small animals   **b** leaves   **c** seeds

5 When is Mountain Chicken Day?
   a 13th December   **b** 13th September   **c** 30th September

3 **Think, pair, share!** Are there any animals in danger in your country? **What do you know about them?**

4 Complete the activities. **AB Page 23**

Lesson 9 Writing **The Big Write AB Pages 24–25**

Lesson 10 | **THE BIG QUESTION REVIEW**

REVIEW VIDEO

1 Watch and answer the questions on the review video. ▷

2 Look back at the unit and say the missing words. Then compare your answers on the Big Question poster.

We can ____ an animal.

We can ____ about animals.

We can see animals from all over the ____ .

Zoos help animals in ____ .

Zoo ____ have an interesting job.

It's fun watching animals when they do ____ or clever things.

3 **Communicate** 💬 Ask and answer.

Which is your favourite answer?

'We can learn about animals.' Meerkats are very interesting.

4 Complete the self-evaluation activities. **AB Page 25**

1 Read and match.

1 Where are they going to go?
2 What are they going to see?
3 What are they going to draw?
4 What are they going to learn about?
5 Where are they going to eat?
6 What are they going to eat?

a They're going to draw pictures of pandas.
b They're going to eat at the café.
c They're going to eat cake and ice cream.
d They're going to go to the safari park.
e They're going to learn about snakes and lizards.
f They're going to see lions and tigers.

2 Look and write.

go to the zoo / go to the beach

They're _going to go to the zoo._

They aren't _____

draw pictures / take photos

They're _____

They aren't _____

play football / play basketball

_____

_____

3 Communicate 💬 Ask and answer about the pictures.

What are they going to do?   They're going to learn about frogs.

4 Write sentences about the pictures in activity 3.

1 _They're going to_ _____   3 _____
2 _____   4 _____

5 Read and write *A* or *B*.

1 I have to wash the elephants. _A_

2 I don't have to feed the monkeys. ____

3 I have to clean the cages. ____

4 I don't have to help the vet. ____

5 I have to observe the lions. ____

6 I have to look after the frogs. ____

6 Write sentences using *has to* or *doesn't have to*.

1 _A waiter has to clean the tables._

2 _He doesn't have to_ _____

3 _____

4 _____

5 _____

6 _____

Clean the tables ✔
Help the cook ✗
Collect the money ✔
Look after the customers ✔
Wash the dishes ✗
Make drinks ✔

7 **Think** Complete the sentences. Use the words in the box or your own ideas.

get up early   help with dinner   do homework   tidy my bedroom
have a shower   wash my hair   look after my brother / sister

On school days, …

I have to _____.

I don't have to _____.

At the weekend, …

I have to _____.

I don't have to _____.

8 **Communicate** Tell your partner your answers to activity 7.

3 What's fun about an after-school club?

Nico's star post ⭐

We can try new activities.

Sing along with Mason

Look with Tess

Fashion World

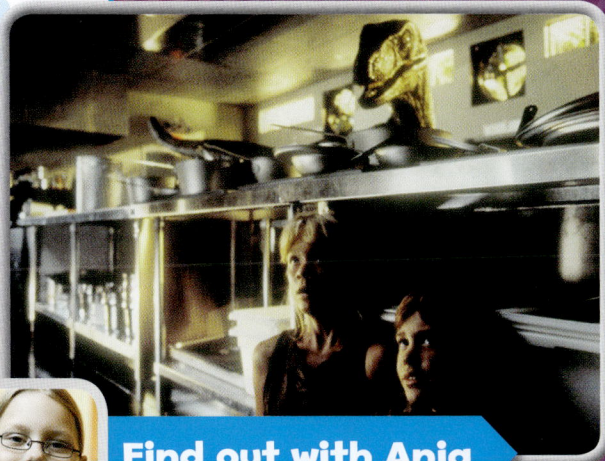

Find out with Ania

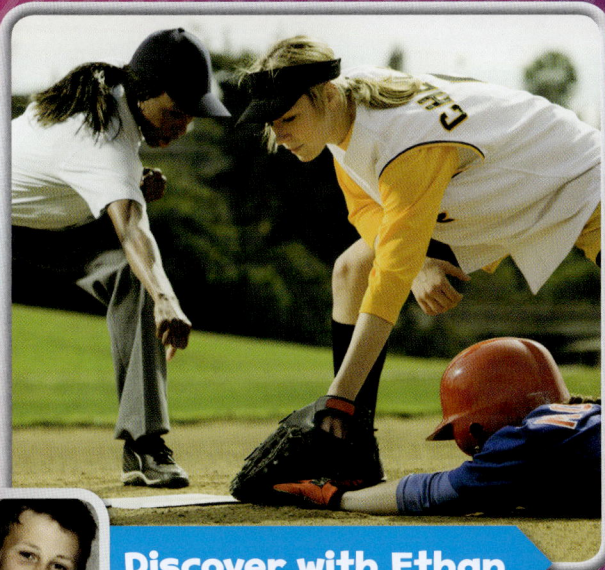

Discover with Ethan

BIG POLL

In after-school clubs, should you ...

have fun or **learn things?**

1 **Look and answer.**

1 What's the Big Question for unit 3?
2 Who are the posts from?
3 What can you see in the pictures?

2 **Which things do you see in the Big Question video? Watch then say.** ▷

- a school
- a castle
- a museum
- a jigsaw
- a climbing wall
- a blue T-shirt
- a rope
- a tunnel
- a horse
- a black shoe

3 **Think** 💭 **What are your answers to the Big Question?**

Keep a list of your answers on the Big Question poster.

UNIT
3
THE BIG QUESTION POSTER
What's fun about an after-school club?

OUR ANSWERS

4 **Answer the Big Poll.**

5 **Watch the Big Question video again.** ▷ **Complete the activities.** AB Page 26

3 Lesson 2 Vocabulary and song

Having a film show is fun.

Mason

1 **Think** 💭 What different kinds of films are there?

2 Listen, point and repeat. 🔊 044
Compare your list with Mason's.

3 Which kind of films do you often, sometimes or never watch?

Mason's list

1 adventure film

2 comedy

3 cartoon

4 wildlife film

5 scary film

6 sci-fi film　　**7** western　　**8** historical film　　**9** romantic film　　**10** musical

4 Listen and sing. 🔊 045

Our club has a film show every week
On Friday afternoons.
There are comedies and adventure films,
But my favourites are cartoons!

Last week we watched a sci-fi film.
They travelled into space.
They found a special rock on Mars
To save the human race.

Chorus

Today we're watching a wildlife film
About some chimpanzees.
They're eating fruit and nuts
And they're playing in the trees.

Chorus

Next week's film is a musical
About a girl who can sing and dance.
She studies at a drama school
And she wants to be a star!

Chorus

5 **Communicate** 💬 Ask and answer. 🔊 046

Do you prefer historical films or romantic films?

Historical films.

Me too.

I don't. I prefer romantic films.

3 Lesson 3 Grammar

1 Listen, read and look at the picture. 🔊 047

Why is Mason's sister behind the sofa?

Hi Nico! Look at my photo! Have a guess! What are we watching?

You're watching a scary film.

Yes! How did you know?

Your sister is hiding behind the sofa. She always hides behind the sofa when she's scared.

You're right! We usually watch comedies.

What are you eating?

Popcorn. I always eat popcorn when I watch a film!

2 Listen and follow. 🔊 048 Ask and answer about Mason.

NOW				I	'm		a comedy.
	are	you		He			a scary film.
What			watching?	She	's	watching	a western.
	is	he					a cartoon.
		she		We	're		

HABIT					I		watch	comedies.
	do	you			We			sci-fi films.
What			usually	watch?		usually		scary films.
	does	he			He		watches	cartoons.
		she			She			

3 Look, listen and read. 🔊 049

What is she watching?

She's watching a western.

What does she usually watch?

She usually watches cartoons.

I know! It's B.

4 Communicate 💬 Play the game.

Present continuous vs present simple

1 Think 💭 What clothes words do you know?

2 Listen, point and repeat. 🔊 051

3 Which clothes do you often wear?
Which do you never wear?

Tess's list

1 wig

2 jeans

3 sandals

4 boots

5 scarf

6 gloves

4 This story is about a fashion show.
Can you guess what Tess and Dev decide to wear?

5 Listen, read and check your ideas. 🔊 052

6 AFTER YOU READ Watch the story video. ▷
Complete the activities. **AB Page 29**

Tess

What's fun about an after-school club?

Fashion shows are popular.

THE BiG Quest **Fashion World**

1 Those people look uncomfortable!

We're in Fashion World.

Challenge
Design an outfit.
The best outfit will be on the **cover** of *Kids' Fashion Magazine*.

2 Brilliant! I love *Kids' Fashion Magazine*.

I don't really like fashion!

Come on. Let's change! I'll wear my favourite outfit. I usually wear it on Saturdays.

3 Oh, is that you, Tess?

Of course it is. Now it's your turn! Change into your favourite outfit.

4 Look! He's wearing fantastic gloves!

5 Welcome, Justin. Your gloves are amazing.

Thank you. I design new gloves every weekend.

6 And now – Rose. How often do you wear a wig?

I wear a different wig every day. I change my wig three times on Sundays.

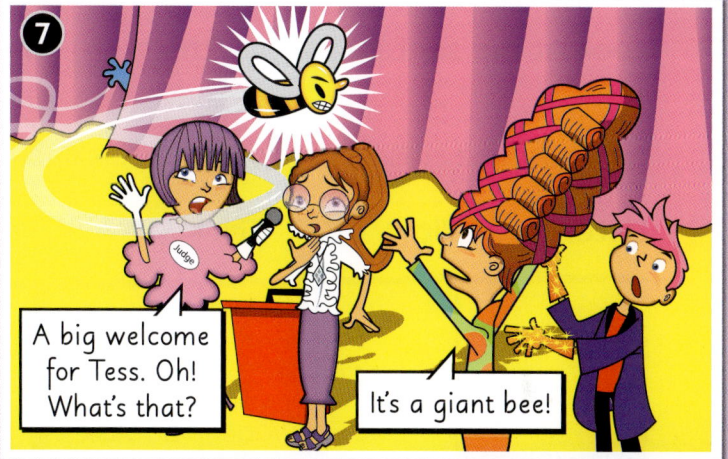

7 A big welcome for Tess. Oh! What's that?

It's a giant bee!

8 I'm scared of bees. Oh no! I can't run in these boots.

My wig! Somebody help me!

Don't worry. I'll catch it. It's only a balloon.

9 Thank you, Dev. You're a hero. And ... what an amazing outfit! Tell us about it.

Er ... um ... My mum buys me a new outfit twice a year.

Only twice a year?

10 Yes, that's right. But I wash my jeans once a week.

Well, we love your outfit. Your jeans are the most comfortable clothes we've seen today.

11 LATER

KIDS' FASHION MAGAZINE

Look, Dev! You're on the cover. You and your jeans are famous now.

LEVEL UP >>>

1 REMEMBER THE STORY Read. Who's speaking?

1 I usually wear my favourite outfit on Saturdays.

2 I design new gloves every weekend.

3 How often do you wear a wig?

4 My mum buys me a new outfit twice a year.

Look!

We can use an adverb and a time expression in the same sentence.
I usually wear my favourite outfit once a week.

2 Look at the sentences from the story. Choose.

a We use the present simple to talk about how often we do something.

b We use the present continuous to talk about how often we do something.

3 Listen and follow. 053 Think Ask your partner about what they wear.

How often	do you	wear buy	gloves? jeans? boots? a scarf? a wig? sandals?	Once a Twice a Three times a Four times a Every	day week month year	in winter. in summer.

4 Think, pair, share! Ask how often your partner buys clothes. Then talk about your partner.

He buys a new T-shirt six times a year.

trousers
shorts
shoes
a jacket
a T-shirt
a sweater

How often do you buy a new T-shirt?

Six times a year.

3 |

Ania

1 Look at the scenes from the film *Jurassic Park*. Read and complete the descriptions with *violent*, *calm* or *tense*. Then listen and check. 🔊 055

2 Listen and read about writing film music. 🔊 056 Why is music important in films?

What's fun about an after-school club?
We can learn about music.

Scene 1

This scene is at the beginning of the film. The island looks ▮▮▮ and beautiful.

Scene 2

In this scene, the velociraptors are hunting the boy and girl. It's a ▮▮▮ moment in the film.

Scene 3

In this scene, Tyrannosaurus Rex turns over the car. The scene is noisy and ▮▮▮.

Writing film music

Listen. Music can be **fast** like this 🔊, or **slow** like this 🔊. This is the **tempo**. Slow music usually sounds calmer than fast music.

Musical notes can be **high** like this 🔊, or **low** like this 🔊. This is the **pitch**. Music with a low pitch often sounds serious. Music with a high pitch can be tense and scary.

Music can be **loud** like this 🔊, or **quiet** like this 🔊. This is the **volume**. Loud music often sounds angrier and more violent than quiet music.

Composers of film music combine tempo, pitch and volume to write music which helps to tell the story.

3 Read the task. Then listen to Ania's music. 🔊 057 Match music A–C with scenes 1–3.

4 Listen again and answer the questions. 🔊 057

1 Is the music for scene 1 calm, tense or violent?
2 What is the tempo of the music for scene 1?
3 Is the music for scene 2 calm, tense or violent?

4 What is the pitch of the music for scene 2?
5 Is the music for scene 3 calm, tense or violent?
6 What is the volume of the music for scene 3?

AFTER-SCHOOL CLUB
Group activity: Film Music
Ania: find or invent some music for the three Jurassic Park scenes.

5 **Think, pair, share!** What kind of music is best to use in these film scenes: *going to bed, driving a fast car, walking down a dark street*?

1 **BEFORE YOU READ** Look at the photos. Where are Ethan and his friends from? How do you know?

What's fun about an after-school club?

End-of-year parties are fantastic!

Ethan

2 Think 💭 What can you do at an after-school club end-of-year party?

3 Read and listen. 🔊 061 Were your ideas in the emails?

After-school club end-of-year party!

From: Jackson Jones   Sent: 5th May (2 days ago)
To: Ethan Roberts, Brooklyn Lopéz, Harper Ward

Hi everybody!

It's nearly the end of the year. It's time to organize our end-of-year party! This year it's on Friday 14th June. Don't forget to tell your families.

What would you like to do at the party? Send me your ideas before Friday 31st May.

Jackson

Re: After-school club end-of-year party!

From: Ethan Roberts   Sent: 7th May (6 hours ago)
To: Jackson Jones

Hi Jackson!

Thanks! I'd like to have a barbecue. We can cook hamburgers and chicken wings. Then we can have ice cream for dessert. My dad says he can help with the food. He does fried green tomatoes on the barbecue. Delicious!

Hope you like my idea!

Ethan

Re: After-school club end-of-year party!

From: Brooklyn Lopéz   Sent: 7th May (5 hours ago)
To: Jackson Jones

Hi Jackson!

Let's have a baseball match. It can be kids against parents! But we want you on our team! My mom will help – she's a baseball referee. She trains the 'Banana Monsters', too. They're in the Little League.

Brooklyn

Re: After-school club end-of-year party!

From: Harper Ward   Sent: 7th May (2 hours ago)
To: Jackson Jones

Hi Jackson!

Why don't we have an awards ceremony? We can have a lot of different awards. How about for the most helpful person and the best sportsperson? We can think of more awards in the club. I'll make the certificates and the medals. We can all vote for the winners!

Harper

---

4 **AFTER YOU READ**
Complete the activities. AB Page 32

Big Values!

Take part in a community event.

1 Listen to Ethan. 🔊 062
Match and say the names and the medals.

Ethan   Harper   Brooklyn

1 MOST HELPFUL PERSON

2 BEST SPORTS PERSON

3 BEST ICE CREAM MAKER

2 Listen again. 🔊 062 Are the sentences true or false? 📄

1 Ethan made chocolate ice cream.
2 Harper always helps tidy up.
3 Harper is good at sports.

4 Brooklyn is a good swimmer.
5 Ethan is in a baseball team.
6 The kids won the baseball match.

3 Think, pair, share! What do you and your friends do at end-of-year parties?

4 Complete the activities. AB Page 33

Lesson 9 Writing   The **Big Write** AB Pages 34–35

Lesson 10   THE BIG QUESTION REVIEW

REVIEW VIDEO

1 Watch and answer the questions on the review video. ▷

2 Look back at the unit and say the missing words.
Then compare your answers on the Big Question poster.

We can try [ ] activities.

We can learn about [ ].

Having a [ ] show is fun.

End-of-year [ ] are fantastic!

[ ] shows are popular.

We have [ ] making things.

3 Communicate 💬 Ask and answer.

Which is your favourite answer?

'Having a film show is fun.' I love watching films with my friends!

4 Complete the self-evaluation activities. AB Page 35

1 Complete the sentences.

| cartoons | ~~comedy~~ | historical | ~~sci-fi~~ | western | wildlife |

1 They're watching a _____comedy_____. They usually watch _____sci-fi_____ films.

2 She usually reads _____ magazines. She's reading a _____ magazine.

3 He's watching a _____. He usually watches _____.

2 Read the answers and write the questions.

1 _What do you usually watch?_ _____   I usually watch comedies.
2 _____   She's watching a musical.
3 _____   He usually reads comic books.
4 _____   They usually watch sci-fi films.
5 _____   I'm reading a historical magazine.
6 _____   He's watching a wildlife film.

3 Think 💭 Find four differences. Write sentences using *eat*, *watch* and *wear*.

Usually

Now

1 _She usually watches films with her dad._   _She's watching a film with her mum._
2 _____   _____
3 _____   _____
4 _____   _____

4 Communicate 💬 Work in pairs. Mime an activity. Your partner guesses.

| eat a sandwich | watch a comedy | make soup | draw a picture | take a photo |

5 Write the answers.

Sundays	Mondays	Tuesdays	Wednesdays	Thursdays	Fridays	Saturdays

New shoes: April and September   New coat: September

> Once a week.   Twice a week.   Three times a week.
> ~~Four times a week.~~   Every day.   Once a year.   Twice a year.

1 How often do you wear jeans?   _Four times a week._ _____

2 How often do you wear a T-shirt?   _____

3 How often do you wear a jacket?   _____

4 How often do you wear a hat?   _____

5 How often do you wear a scarf?   _____

6 How often do you buy new shoes?   _____

7 How often do you buy a new coat?   _____

6 Write questions with *How often*.

1 (write) (emails)   _How often do you write emails?_ _____

2 (buy) (toys)   _____

3 (eat) (ice cream)   _____

4 (read) (comics)   _____

5 (go to) (a sports centre) _____

7 **Communicate** 💬 Ask and answer the questions from activity 6 with your partner.

8 Write sentences about you and your partner. 📝

I write emails every day, but Millie writes emails twice a week.

1 **BEFORE YOU READ** Look at the headings and pictures in the reviews of *Black Beauty*. Answer.

1 What kind of animal is Black Beauty?
2 Who is the author of *Black Beauty*?
3 Who liked the book? Who didn't like the book?

2 Read and listen. 🔊064 Check your ideas.

3 **AFTER YOU READ** Ask and answer about the characters in the book.

> Who's Joe?
> He's a groom.
> What's Joe like?
> He's kind.

4 Complete the activities. **AB Page 36**

Black Beauty by Anna Sewell

Reviews

Review by **Raj Gupta** ⭐⭐⭐⭐⭐

Black Beauty is the perfect book for children who love animals. It's set in England in the 19th century. There weren't any cars, taxis or tractors in those days. Horses pulled carriages, cabs and carts. Black Beauty was a working horse and this book is the story of his life. It's sometimes very sad, but it's always very interesting.

Black Beauty grew up on a farm with his mother and some other young horses. When he was four years old, he had to start to work. He had a lot of different jobs. First, he pulled a carriage for a rich family who lived in a big house. Later, he pulled a cab in London, and at the end of his life he pulled a heavy cart. Some of his owners were kind, and some of them were cruel. It was a hard life, but finally Black Beauty went to a good home.

My favourite horse character is called Merrylegs. He's a pretty little horse, and he's always happy. I really like Jerry the cab driver, too. He's kind to Black Beauty and his other horses.

This is a fantastic book. It's quite long, but it's never boring. It's a great story, and there's also a good message in this book: be kind to animals.

1 **Think** 💭 **Read the reviews again. Answer.**

  1 What words does Raj use to describe the book?
  2 What words does Ella use to describe the book?

2 **Think, pair, share!** **Would you like to read** *Black Beauty*? **Why? Why not?**

3 **Complete the activities.** **AB Page 37** ▶

Review by **Ella Stephens** ⭐⭐☆☆☆

Black Beauty was a beautiful horse, but he had a terrible life. He lived in England about 150 years ago. Horses had to work in those days, and people were often cruel to them. This book is about Black Beauty's life. It's a very sad book.

When Black Beauty was young, he lived on a farm with his mother. Then he went to work at a big house and made friends with two horses, Ginger and Merrylegs. Later, Black Beauty had lots of different jobs in London. He had to work very hard. He had to pull heavy carts. In one job, his groom stole his food and didn't look after him well. Finally, a farmer bought him and Black Beauty went back to a farm, where he was happy.

My favourite horse character is Ginger. She's a strong, honest horse. She's angry with humans because they aren't always kind to horses. One of the best human characters is the groom, Joe Green. Joe loves horses and always looks after them very well.

I think the author wrote this book to send a message to the world. She wanted to show how people were cruel to horses. This is an important message, but I didn't like the book. I'm not saying it's a bad book, but it isn't for me. It's long, it's often very sad and it's sometimes boring.

Glossary

This is a family **carriage**. The man looking after the horse is a **groom**.

This is a **cab**, or taxicab.

This is a farm **cart**.

Draw a giant animal

1 **Think** 💭 Number the project stages in order in your notebook. 📝
Then look at pages 46–49 and check. **WHOLE CLASS**

a Choose one animal for your poster.

b Present your drawing to your class.

c Think about how to make a small picture bigger.

d Draw your giant animal.

e Find out which animals your group wants to draw.

f Decide how your project group is going to work together.

Think about it

2 **Think** 💭 Answer the questions. **WHOLE CLASS**

1 Do you know the names of any insects?
2 Do you know the names of any pond animals?
3 Do you know the names of any small sea animals?

3 **Communicate** 💬 Look at the pictures and answer. **PROJECT GROUP**

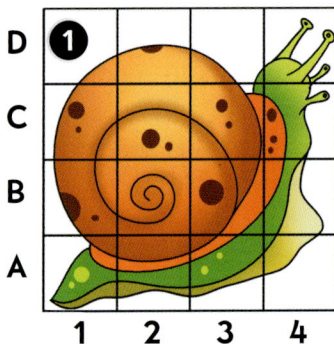

1 What can you see in picture 1?
2 How many squares are there in the grid on picture 1?
3 How big is one square on the grid?   **a** 1 cm x 1 cm   **b** 2 cm x 2 cm
4 Picture 2 is the same as one square in picture 1. Which square?
5 How big is picture 2?   **a** 1 cm x 1 cm   **b** 5 cm x 5 cm
6 Imagine you have copied all the squares in picture 1 and put them together to make a new picture. How big is the new picture?   **a** 10 cm x 10 cm   **b** 20 cm x 20 cm

4 Find out which animals your group wants to draw.
Make notes in your Activity Book. **AB Page 38 Activity 1** **PROJECT GROUP**

Pupil 1 Which flying insect would your group like to draw?

 dragonfly

 butterfly

Pupil 2 Which land insect would your group like to draw?

 ant

 grasshopper

Pupil 3 Which sea animal would your group like to draw?

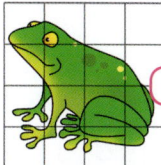 crab

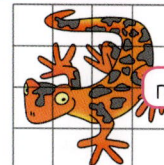 seahorse

Pupil 4 Which pond animal would your group like to draw?

frog

newt

Choose

5 **Collaborate** Tell your group your information.
Choose one animal to draw. **AB Page 38 Activity 2** **PROJECT GROUP**

Two of us want to draw a butterfly and two of us want to draw a crab.

OK. We have to vote. Hands up if you want to draw a butterfly!

OK. Let's draw a butterfly with a lot of different colours!

6 Look, listen and match. Then listen and repeat. 🔊 065 **WHOLE CLASS**

English in use

We use *Shall I ...?* to offer to do something.

❶ We have to make sixteen squares of paper of 30 cm x 30 cm.

❷ We have to decide who is going to cut out the squares.

❸ We have to decide who is going to copy each square.

I've got a ruler. Shall I draw the squares?

I've got some scissors. Shall I cut out the squares?

I'm good at drawing. Shall I copy the squares in rows A and B?

ⓐ **ⓑ** **ⓒ**

7 Listen and follow. 🔊 066 Then look at the pictures and say. **PROJECT GROUP**

Shall	I	copy the squares in rows C and D?	Yes, OK.
		choose the colours?	Great!
		colour the squares?	Well, I'd prefer to do that.
		stick the squares on the wall?	

❶ **❷** **❸**

8 What can you learn from this project? Complete the questions in your Activity Book and write answers for your animal. **AB Page 38 Activity 3** **PROJECT GROUP**

How many legs has a crab got?

Has a crab got eyes?

What colours can a crab's shell be?

Make

9 **Create** 💡 Follow the steps. Make your giant animal. **PROJECT GROUP**

Step 1: four pupils
Decide how big you want your animal to be. Decide who is going to draw the squares and who is going to cut them out. Draw and cut out the squares of paper. You need 16 squares.

Step 2: four pupils
Decide who is going to copy part of the animal on each square, and who is going to colour each square. Then draw and colour in the squares.

Step 3: four pupils
Stick the squares onto the wall or a big piece of paper.

Present

10 Present your giant animal to your class. Then answer questions from your class. **WHOLE CLASS**

11 **Think** 💭 Think about the project and answer the questions. **WHOLE CLASS**

1 What did you enjoy about this project?

2 What did you find difficult?

3 Were you surprised by anything?

4 How could you do the project better next time?

4 What's exciting about exploring?

Junior's star post ⭐

You can explore your own city.

Sing along with Sophie

Look with Dev

Bird World

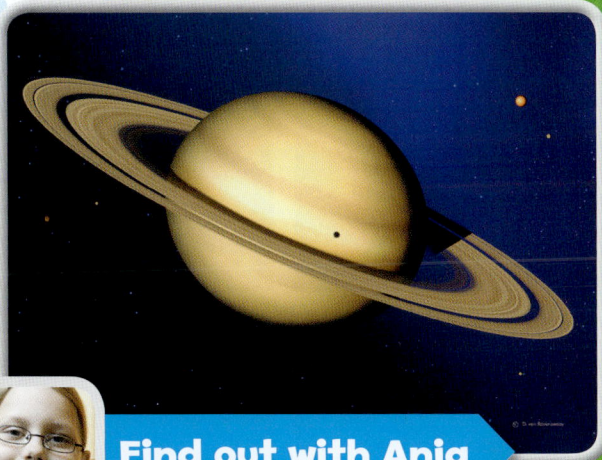

Find out with Ania

Discover with Camila

BIG POLL
Would you prefer to explore places ...
on Earth or **in space?**

1 **Look and answer.**

1 What's the Big Question for unit 4?
2 Who are the posts from?
3 What can you see in the pictures?

2 **Which things do you see in the Big Question video? Watch then say.** ▷

- a red bus
- an orange house
- a mountain
- a table
- a forest
- a beach
- the sea
- a sea lion
- a statue
- a boat

3 **Think** 💭 **What are your answers to the Big Question?**

Keep a list of your answers on the Big Question poster.

UNIT **4** | what's exciting about exploring?
THE BIG QUESTION POSTER
OUR ANSWERS

4 **Answer the Big Poll.**

5 **Watch the Big Question video again.** ▷ **Complete the activities.** AB Page 40 ▷

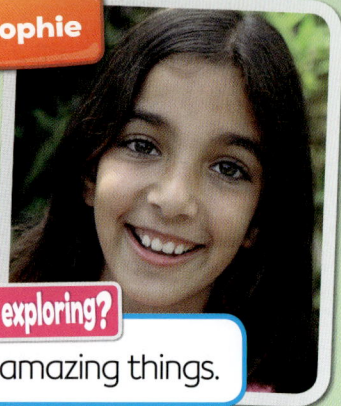

Sophie

1 Think 💭 What kind of things do explorers do?

2 Listen, point and repeat. 🔊 068
Compare your list with Sophie's.

3 Say where in the world you can do these things.

What's exciting about exploring?
Explorers do amazing things.

Sophie's list

1 climb a cliff   **2** climb a volcano   **3** canoe on a river   **4** explore a cave   **5** explore a jungle

6 explore an island   **7** trek across a desert   **8** walk under a waterfall   **9** walk on the moon   **10** dive near a coral reef

4 Listen and sing. 🔊 069

Ella the brave explorer
Gave us a talk at school.
She's been on great adventures.
An explorer's life is cool!

She's explored a dangerous jungle,
And studied the people there.
She's canoed on muddy rivers
With piranhas everywhere.

Chorus

She's explored a rocky island,
And lived there in a cave.
She's climbed a live volcano.
She's really very brave!

Chorus

She's travelled into space,
And walked on the moon up there.
She's trekked across a desert.
She's explored everywhere!

Chorus

5 Communicate 💬 Ask and answer. 🔊 070

Would you like to walk under a waterfall?

Yes, I would.

Would you like to climb a volcano?

No, I wouldn't.

1 **Listen, read and look at the picture.** 🔊 071

Where is Ella in the photo?
When was she there?

Look at this photo of Ella Dawson with my friend Lucy. She came to our school today.

Really? I saw her on TV last week. She's a great explorer.

That's right. She's trekked across a desert in Australia. And she's dived near a coral reef there, too.

The Great Barrier Reef in Australia! We've studied that at school. It's amazing.

She told us some fantastic stories. She's travelled everywhere!

Everywhere? To the Antarctic?

OK. She hasn't travelled to the Antarctic. But she's thinking of it!

2 **Listen and follow.** 🔊 072
Say sentences about your friends and family.

He She	's has	dived near a coral reef. climbed a cliff. walked on the moon.
	hasn't	canoed on a river. explored a cave. walked under a waterfall.

3 **Look, listen and read.** 🔊 073

He's explored a cave.

It's Marco or Chris. Go on.

He hasn't dived near a coral reef.

I know! It's Marco.

4 **Communicate** 💬 **Play the game.**

	Marco	Chris	Cheng	Abu
	✔	✔	✘	✘
	✘	✔	✔	✘
	✔	✘	✘	✔
	✘	✘	✔	✔

1 Think 💭 What names of birds do you know?

2 Listen, point and repeat. 🔊 075

3 Which of these birds have you seen? Which haven't you seen?

What's exciting about exploring?
Explorers find unknown animals.

Dev

THE **BiG Quest** Bird World

Dev's list

1 swan   **2** eagle

3 hummingbird   **4** peacock

5 parrot   **6** vulture

4 BEFORE YOU READ This is a story about finding an unknown bird. What do you think it looks like?

5 Listen, read and check your ideas. 🔊 076

6 AFTER YOU READ Watch the story video. ▷ Complete the activities. **AB Page 43**

1 We're in Bird World!

Look, Dev! Here comes the challenge. It's coming down the zip wire!

2 **Challenge**
Find the **Little Tweeter**.
It's as small as a hummingbird.
It's as colourful as a parrot.
It's as beautiful as a peacock.
Win a **zip wire trip** through Bird World!

3 The Little Tweeter is a bird. How can we catch it?

I don't know. Oh look! Here's Lucky with a clue. It's a net!

Tess　　**Dev**

1 **REMEMBER THE STORY** Read and match.

1　What does it　　　　**a**　a parrot.
2　It's as colourful as　　**b**　look like?
3　It's as ugly as　　　　**c**　a hummingbird.
4　He isn't as small as　　**d**　a vulture.

2 Look at the sentences from the story.　Choose.

a　We use *as* + adjective + *as* to say that two things are the same.
b　We use *as* + adjective + *as* to say that two things are different.

Look!

These two sentences have the same meaning.
He isn't as small as a hummingbird. **=** *He's bigger than a hummingbird.*

3 Listen and follow. 🔊077 **Think** 💭 Say true sentences about the Little Tweeter.

It	's		big small		a swan. an eagle.
He	is	as	colourful beautiful	as	a hummingbird. a peacock.
She	isn't		ugly noisy		a parrot. a vulture.

4 **Think, pair, share!** Compare your friends and family.
Then talk about your partner.

tall
old
fit
strong
funny
clever

He's as fit as his friend.

She isn't as tall as her brother.

I'm not as tall as my brother.

I'm as fit as my friend.

Ania

1 BEFORE YOU READ Look at the photos. Which planet is this? Do you know the names of the spacecraft?

2 Look at the timeline and read. Check your answers.

What's exciting about exploring?
We can explore other planets.

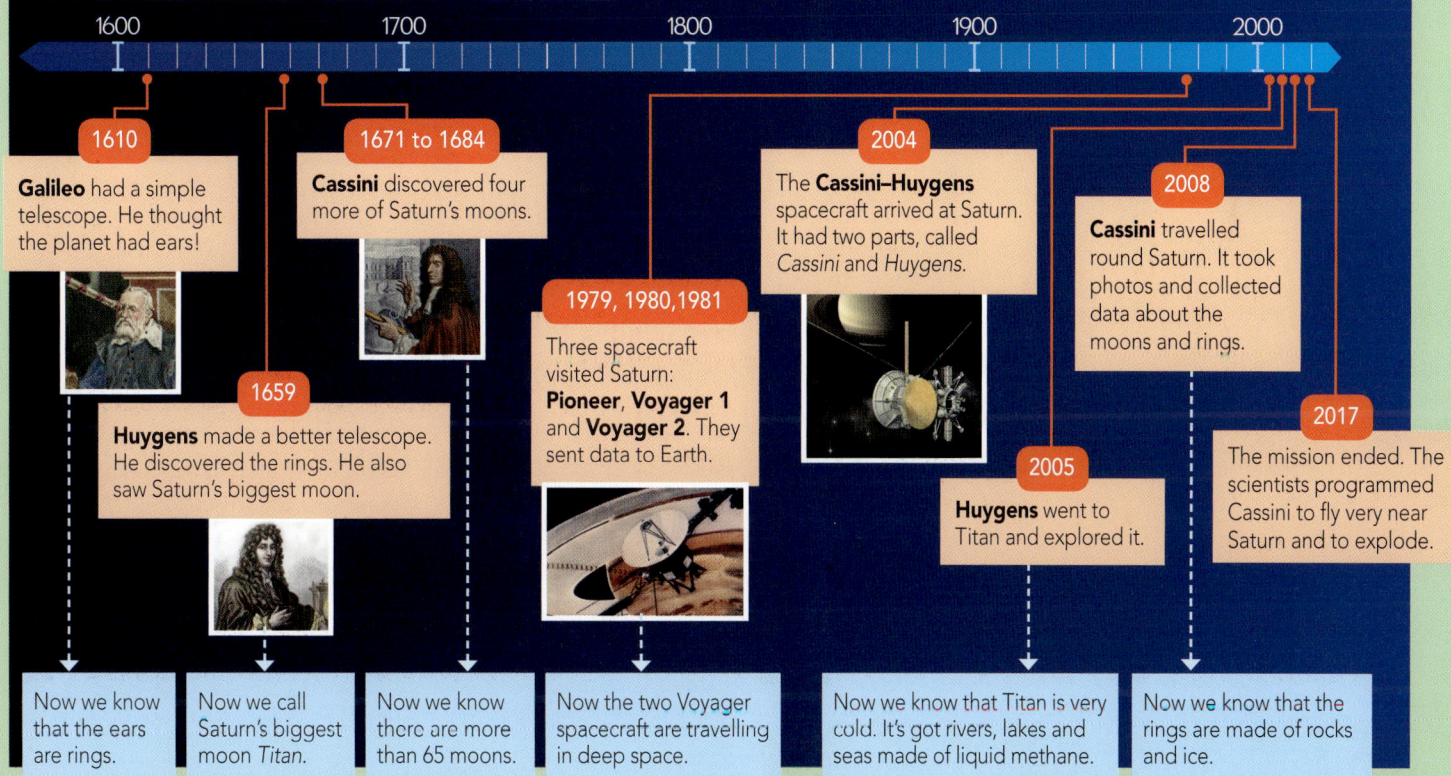

rings

Saturn is the sixth planet from the Earth. It's the second-biggest planet in the solar system. It's made of gas. How do we know this? We can't go to Saturn, but we can explore it with telescopes and spacecraft.

1600 — 1700 — 1800 — 1900 — 2000

1610
Galileo had a simple telescope. He thought the planet had ears!

1671 to 1684
Cassini discovered four more of Saturn's moons.

2004
The **Cassini–Huygens** spacecraft arrived at Saturn. It had two parts, called *Cassini* and *Huygens*.

2008
Cassini travelled round Saturn. It took photos and collected data about the moons and rings.

1979, 1980, 1981
Three spacecraft visited Saturn: **Pioneer**, **Voyager 1** and **Voyager 2**. They sent data to Earth.

1659
Huygens made a better telescope. He discovered the rings. He also saw Saturn's biggest moon.

2005
Huygens went to Titan and explored it.

2017
The mission ended. The scientists programmed Cassini to fly very near Saturn and to explode.

Now we know that the ears are rings.

Now we call Saturn's biggest moon *Titan*.

Now we know there are more than 65 moons.

Now the two Voyager spacecraft are travelling in deep space.

Now we know that Titan is very cold. It's got rivers, lakes and seas made of liquid methane.

Now we know that the rings are made of rocks and ice.

3 Read again. Are the sentences true or false? Say.

1. Galileo discovered that Saturn had rings in 1610.
2. Huygens' telescope was stronger than Galileo's telescope.
3. Cassini discovered 65 of Saturn's moons.
4. Spacecraft started to visit Saturn in the 1990s.
5. Cassini went to Titan in 2005.
6. The rivers and lakes on Titan are made of water.
7. The Cassini–Huygens mission ended in 2008.

Glossary

explode

4 Think, pair, share! What other planets do you know about?

Camila

1 BEFORE YOU READ Look at the dates of the explorer's diary entries. Why are the pictures drawings, not photos?

2 Think Ask questions about this explorer.

3 Read and listen. 079
Does the diary answer your questions?

What's exciting about exploring?
Explorers make discoveries.

16th June 1799
Today has been a very strange day. I was in Cumaná with my friends. We met an explorer called Alexander Humboldt. He wants to explore the Orinoco River. He needs a helper. He can't speak our language, but I can speak Spanish and English. I'm going to go with him. I'm very excited!

19th February 1800
We're exploring the Orinoco River with Mr Humboldt. He's interested in everything. Today we found some electric eels in the river. Mr Humboldt was very surprised. He didn't know these animals. We caught some eels for him. He picked one up and got a terrible electric shock. He nearly died! Then he opened the eel with a knife. He wanted to discover how it worked.

23rd June 1802
Today we climbed the Chimborazo Volcano. Mr Humboldt always carries scientific instruments with him. He discovered that the volcano is 5,878 metres high. He was happy because it's the highest that a European has climbed. It was very dangerous, because there was ice at the top. I was scared, but Mr Humboldt laughed!

Big Values!
Take an interest in the natural world around you.

4 AFTER YOU READ
Complete the activities. AB Page 46

4 Lesson 8 Culture

1 Listen to Camila talking to her aunt about a trip in Venezuela. 🔊 080 Answer.

Is it easy to go to Angel Falls?

2 Listen again. 🔊 080 Order the sentences. 📝

a They got out of the canoe.
b They camped in the jungle.
c They saw flowers, frogs and parrots.
d They started their trip in a canoe.
e They saw the highest waterfall in the world.
f They saw fish and snakes.

3 **Think, pair, share!** What amazing geographical features are there in your area?

4 Complete the activities. **AB Page 47**

Lesson 9 Writing   The **Big Write** AB Pages 48–49

Lesson 10   **THE BIG QUESTION REVIEW**

1 Watch and answer the questions on the review video. ▷

REVIEW VIDEO

2 Look back at the unit and say the missing words. Then compare your answers on the Big Question poster.

You can explore your own ____ .

We can explore other ____ .

Explorers do ____ things.

Explorers make ____ .

Explorers find unknown ____ .

Explorers need to be ____ .

3 **Communicate** 💬 Ask and answer.

Which is your favourite answer?

'We can explore other planets.' I'd like to go to Mars!

4 Complete the self-evaluation activities. **AB Page 49**

1 Write *'s* or *hasn't*.

1 She _'s_____ climbed a mountain.

2 He _____ walked under a waterfall.

3 She _____ canoed on a river.

4 He _____ explored a jungle.

5 He _____ trekked across a desert.

6 He _____ dived in the sea.

7 She _____ walked under a waterfall.

8 She _____ trekked across a desert.

2 **Think** Think about a friend and tick ✔ or cross ✗ the things he / she has done.

climbed a cliff	☐	climbed a tall building	☐
explored a city	☐	dived in the sea	☐
walked in a desert	☐	trekked in the mountains	☐

3 Write sentences about the things your friend has and hasn't done.

1 _____

2 _____

3 _____

4 _____

5 _____

6 _____

4 Think 💭 Read and circle.

1 It's as large as a peacock. It isn't as colourful as a parrot. hummingbird (swan)
2 It's as fast as an eagle. It isn't as beautiful as a swan. vulture peacock
3 It's as colourful as a peacock. It isn't as small as a hummingbird. parrot vulture
4 It's as fast as a vulture. It isn't as colourful as a parrot. hummingbird eagle

5 Think 💭 Invent, draw and colour a new bird. Give it a name.

6 Write sentences about your bird.

1 loud / parrot — *It isn't as loud as a parrot.*
2 beautiful / swan
3 small / hummingbird
4 fast / eagle
5 colourful / peacock
6 heavy / vulture

7 Communicate 💬 Tell your partner about your bird.

5 How can we help at home?

Jack's star post ⭐

We can cook a meal.

Sing along with Lily

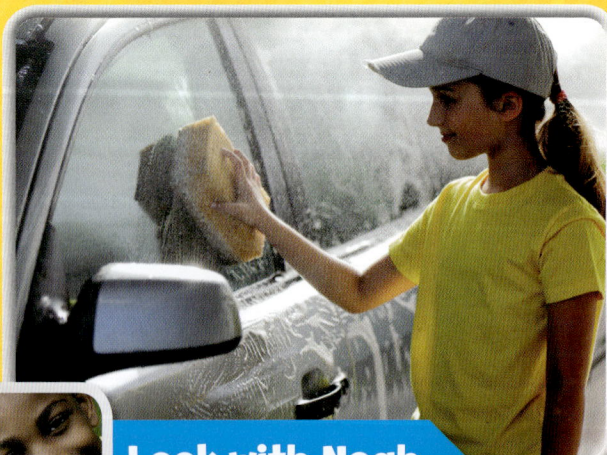

Look with Noah

Robot World

title **Do you ever lay the table?**

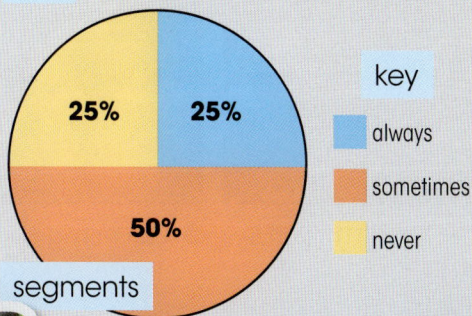

key
- always
- sometimes
- never

25%   25%

50%

segments

Find out with Sophie

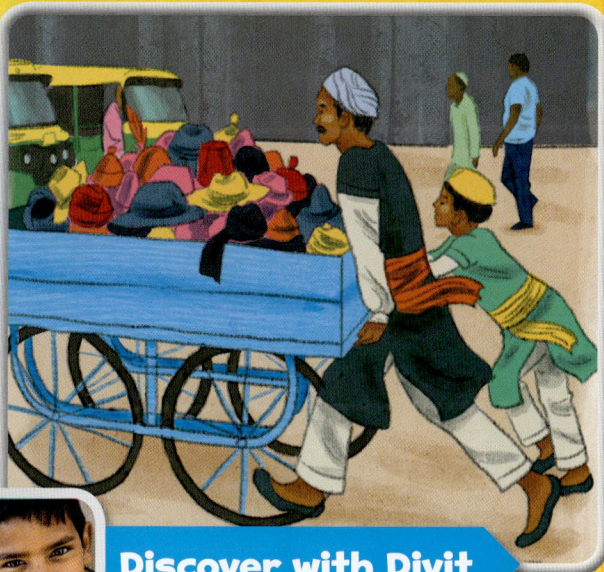

Discover with Divit

BIG POLL

Do you prefer helping ...
indoors or **outdoors** ?

1 Look and answer.

1 What's the Big Question for unit 5?
2 Who are the posts from?
3 What can you see in the pictures?

2 Which things do you see in the Big Question video? Watch then say. ▷

- a kitchen
- red cupboards
- a courgette
- carrots
- mushrooms
- chicken
- spinach
- sweetcorn
- strawberries
- a spoon

3 Think 💭 What are your answers to the Big Question?

Keep a list of your answers on the Big Question poster.

UNIT 5   THE BIG QUESTION POSTER
How can we help at home?

OUR ANSWERS

4 Answer the Big Poll.

5 Watch the Big Question video again. ▷ Complete the activities. **AB Page 50**

5 **Lesson 2** Vocabulary and song

Lily

1 **Think** 💭 What indoor chores can you think of?

2 Listen, point and repeat. 🔊 083
Compare your list with Lily's.

3 Say who does these chores in your house.

How can we help at home?
We can put away our own things.

Lily's list

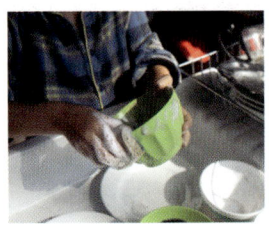

1 make my bed   **2** wash up   **3** lay the table   **4** feed my pets   **5** clean my shoes

6 tidy my room   **7** put away the shopping   **8** vacuum the floor   **9** take out the rubbish   **10** load the dishwasher

4 Listen and sing. 🔊 084

Clean your shoes!
Vacuum the floor!
Make your bed!
Have you finished your chores?

Yes, I have. Yes, I have.
I've cleaned my shoes,
I've vacuumed the floor
And I've made my bed.

OK, now your chores are done,
Go out and play and have some fun!
(x2)

Tidy your room!
Put away those toys!
Feed the fish!
Have you finished your chores?

Yes, I have. Yes, I have.
I've tidied my room,
I've put away my toys
And I've fed the fish.

Chorus

5 **Communicate** 💬 Ask and answer. 🔊 085

Do you ever wash up?

Do you ever clean your shoes?

Yes, sometimes.

No, never.

5

1 **Listen, read and look at the picture.** 🔊 086

What's Lily going to do now?

Hi Jack! Look at my cake. Do you like it?

Yes, it looks yummy. Have you finished your homework?

No, I haven't. I've been busy. I've cleaned the kitchen, loaded the dishwasher and taken out the rubbish.

Amazing! Have you tidied your room, too?

Yes, I have. And my brother has made his bed and tidied his room.

Wow!

He's vacuumed the floors, too.

That's great. But why?

It's a surprise for Mum. It's her birthday today! I have to go now! We're going to decorate the cake.

2 **Listen and follow.** 🔊 087 **Ask and answer about what you've done today.**

Have	you	loaded the dishwasher? made your bed? fed the pets?	Yes, I have. No, I haven't.
Has	he	put away the shopping? laid the table? taken out the rubbish?	Yes, he has. No, he hasn't.

3 **Look, listen and read.** 🔊 088

Has he washed up today?

Yes, he has.

OK. It's Eric or Chen. Has he laid the table?

No, he hasn't.

I know! It's Chen!

4 **Communicate** 💬 **Play the game.**

Eric   Hakan

Chen   Ata

1 Think 💭 What chores would you like a housework robot to do?

2 Listen, point and repeat. 🔊 090

3 Which of these chores do you do? Which don't you do?

How can we help at home?

We can invent a robot to do chores.

Noah

Noah's list

1 water the plants

2 wash the windows

3 sweep the patio

4 cut the grass

5 wash the car

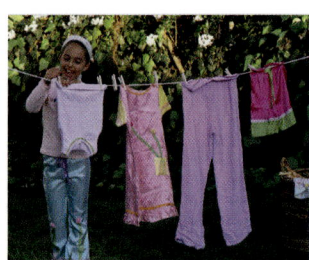

6 hang out the clothes

4 **BEFORE YOU READ** This is a story about a housework robot. What problems do you think he has?

5 Listen, read and check your ideas. 🔊 091

6 **AFTER YOU READ** Watch the story video. ▶ Complete the activities. **AB Page 53**

THE BIG Quest

Robot World

① Where are we?

It's a workshop. These are robot parts. We're in Robot World.

② **Challenge**
Make a robot to wash the car, hang out the clothes and water the plants.
Win an afternoon with Hetty, the robot home help!

Great! We have to make a robot. I love making things.

③ We've finished!

He's cute. Let's call him Robotini. Let's try him out.

4. **Start!**

I'll programme him. Wash the car. Hang out the clothes. Water the plants.

5. **Great! He's working.**

Let's go and play.

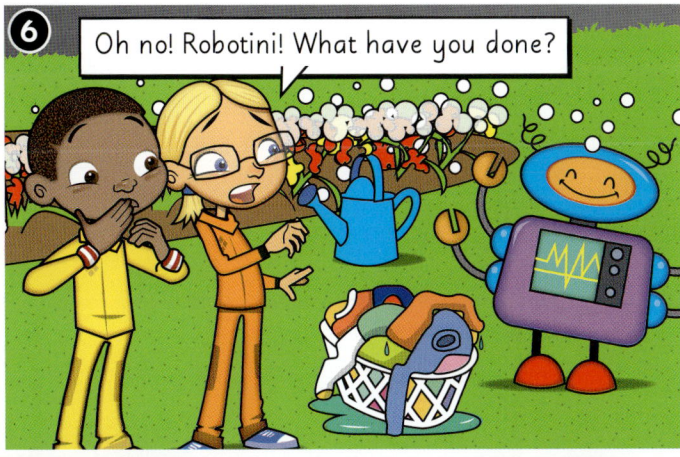

6. Oh no! Robotini! What have you done?

7. I've washed the plants.

Oh no!

8. I've watered the clothes.

Oh no!

9. Don't tell me! You've hung out the car?

I'm sorry. I haven't hung out the car. I can only carry 10 kg.

Max 10kg

10. Wait a minute! Look at this!

It was Trick! He's changed the programmes.

11. Done! I've corrected the programmes.

Off you go, Robotini!

12. He's done the chores. Well done, Robotini!

And we've won the prize.

LEVEL UP >>>

1 **REMEMBER THE STORY** Read. Who is speaking?

1 I've watered the clothes.

2 I haven't hung out the car.

3 I've corrected the programmes.

4 We've won the prize.

Ania **Robotini** **Noah**

2 **Look at the sentences from the story. Choose.**

a We use *I've* + past participle for a past action with a present result, but we don't say when it happened.

b We use *I've* + past participle for a past action that happened a long time ago.

3 **Listen and follow.** 🔊 092 **Think** 💭 **You are Robotini. Mime doing a chore. Then say.**

I / We	've	watered the plants. washed the car. swept the patio.
	haven't	cut the grass. washed the windows. hung out the clothes.

Look!

We make the present perfect with the past participle.

Regular verbs
wash   washed   washed

Irregular verbs
hang   hung   hung
do   did   done

4 **Think, pair, share!** **Find three other students who have or haven't done the same things as you today. Then tell your group.**

put away my toys   had a maths lesson   had breakfast
drunk a glass of milk   read a story   watched TV

We've put away our toys today. We've had a maths lesson. We haven't drunk a glass of milk.

I've put away my toys.

Me too!

I've had a maths lesson.

Me too!

I haven't drunk a glass of milk.

Me neither!

How can we help at home?
We all help in different ways.

Sophie

1 Read and answer. How many charts has Sophie used?

My survey

I wanted to find out how the children in my class help at home.
I did a survey. I wrote the questions and answers in a tally chart.

I = one child   ⊞ = five children

Do you ever ...	Always	Sometimes	Never
make your bed?	III	⊞ II	II
feed your pet?	⊞	IIII	III
lay the table?	III	⊞ I	III
water the plants?	II	⊞ III	II

The results

I've presented the results in two different ways: in four pie charts and on a bar chart.

title **Do you ever lay the table?**

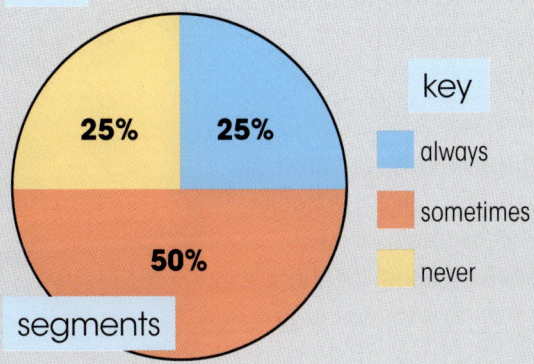

25% 25%
50%

key
■ always
■ sometimes
■ never

segments

title **How do the children in class 4A help at home?**

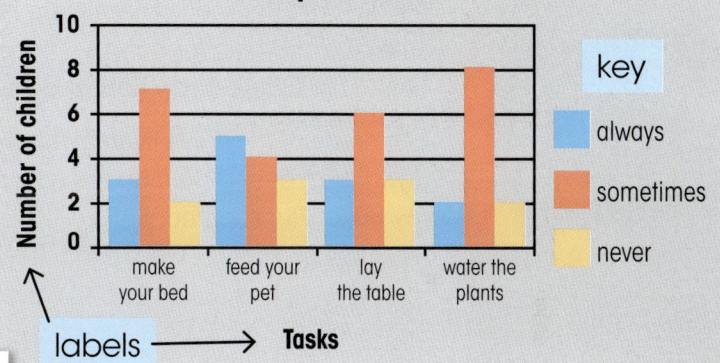

Number of children

make your bed · feed your pet · lay the table · water the plants

labels → **Tasks**

key
■ always
■ sometimes
■ never

This is one of my pie charts. It shows different answers to one question. The key shows the colours I've used for each answer.

My bar chart shows the answers to all the questions in my survey.

2 Read and look at the charts. Answer.

1 How many questions are there on the tally chart?
2 How many children answered the questions?
3 How many possible answers are there on the tally chart?
4 What colour represents *sometimes* on the pie and bar charts?
5 What is the title of the pie chart?
6 What colour is the biggest segment of the pie chart?
7 What is the title of the bar chart?
8 How many children sometimes feed their pet?

3 **Think, pair, share!** Which chart shows the results of the survey better? Why?

How can we help at home?

Sometimes we can help by giving good ideas.

Divit

1 **BEFORE YOU READ** Look at the pictures. Who is the story about?

2 **Think** Why do you think the man is jumping up and down in picture 4?

3 Read, listen and check your ideas. 🔊 094

What a monkey sees, a monkey does

Once upon a time, a long time ago, there was a hat maker called Raj. One day Raj and his son Samar got up early to go to market. Samar helped his father to carry all the hats for sale out of the house. They put them in their little cart. It was time to go. They put on their own hats and set off for market.

Suddenly there was an accident. The cart fell over and all the hats fell out onto the road. There were hats for old men and hats for little girls and hats for babies. There were sports caps and riding hats. There were straw hats and woolly hats.

Hundreds of monkeys lived in the trees by the road. They climbed down the trees, picked up the hats and put them on! 'Give me back my hats!' Raj shouted. He picked up a stick and he waved it at the monkeys. But ... what a monkey sees, a monkey does. All the monkeys picked up sticks and waved them at Raj. Samar watched and listened.

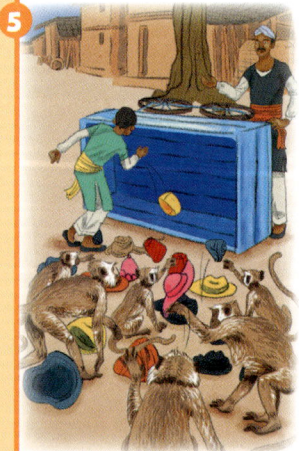

'Give me back my hats!' Raj shouted again. He jumped up and down and he started to cry. But ... what a monkey sees, a monkey does. The monkeys jumped up and down. They started to cry. Samar watched and listened and thought.

'It's no good. We've lost our hats,' said Raj. 'Come on, Samar. Let's go home.' But Samar had an idea. He took off his hat and he threw it into the cart. 'What are you doing?' said Raj. 'Look!' said Samar. What a monkey sees, a monkey does. The monkeys took off their hats and threw them into the cart.

'Well done, Samar,' said Raj. And they continued to market.

4 **AFTER YOU READ**

Complete the activities. **AB Page 56**

Big Values!

It's important to think about the result of your action before you do something.

1 **Listen to Divit.** 🔊 095 **Answer.**

Who does more chores, Divit or his sister Meena?

2 **Listen again.** 🔊 095 **Answer the questions.**
Say *Divit*, *Meena*, or *Divit and Meena*.

1 Who has football practice three days a week?
2 Who helps in the kitchen?
3 Who takes Divit's dad his *tiffin* every day?
4 Who lays the table?
5 Who washes up?
6 Who sweeps the patio?
7 Who tidies the house?
8 Who has to do homework every day?

3 **Think, pair, share!** Do girls and boys help in different ways in your country?

4 **Complete the activities.** AB Page 57

Lesson 9 Writing The **Big Write** AB Pages 58–59

Lesson 10 **THE BIG QUESTION REVIEW**

1 **Watch and answer the questions on the review video.** ▶

REVIEW VIDEO

2 **Look back at the unit and say the missing words.**
Then compare your answers on the Big Question poster.

We can [ ] a meal.

We all help in [ ] ways.

We can put [ ] our own things.

Sometimes we can help by giving good [ ].

We can invent a [ ] to do chores.

We can do [ ] other people don't like.

3 **Communicate** 💬 **Ask and answer.**

Which is your favourite answer?

'We all help in different ways.' I always cut the grass.

4 **Complete the self-evaluation activities.** AB Page 59

1 Look and read. Write *Yes, she has* or *No, she hasn't.*

Lucy's bedroom

1 Has Lucy made her bed?

Yes, she has.

2 Has she tidied her desk?

_____

3 Has she put away her clothes?

_____

4 Has she taken out the rubbish?

_____

2 Complete the questions and write the answers.

1 (clean) _____*Have*_____ you_____*cleaned*_____ your shoes?

*No, I haven't.*_____

2 (feed) _____ you _____ the cat?

_____

3 (lay) _____ she _____ the table?

_____

4 (load) _____ he _____ the dishwasher?

_____

3 Communicate 💬 Write questions for your partner using the information from activity 1. Ask and answer about today.

1 *Have you made your bed today?*

2 _____

3 _____

4 _____

Have you made your bed today? Yes, I have.

4 **Think** Find the differences. Write about picture B.

A

B

| cut | hung out | put away | swept | washed | watered |

1 _____We've cut_____ the grass.
2 _____ the windows.
3 _____ the clothes.
4 _____ the plants.
5 _____ the toys.
6 _____ the patio.

5 **Think** Look at the pictures. Tick ✔ the things you've done this week. Write sentences.

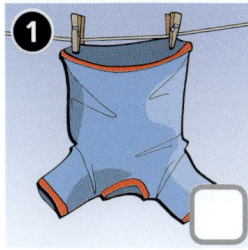

1 □   2 □   3 □   4 □   5 □

1 _I haven't hung out the clothes._____
2 _____
3 _____
4 _____
5 _____

6 **Communicate** Talk to your partner. Find answers from activity 5 that are the same.

Amelia's star post ⭐

A trip to the beach is great.

Sing along with Tess

Look with Ben

Freddy's Funfair World

Find out with Mason

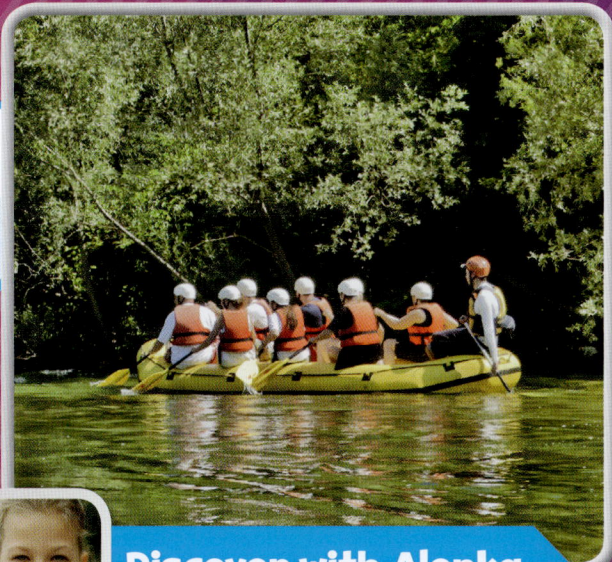

Discover with Alenka

BIG POLL

Do you prefer a day out with ...
your family
or
your school friends?

1 Look and answer.

1 What's the Big Question for unit 6?
2 Who are the posts from?
3 What can you see in the pictures?

2 Which things do you see in the Big Question video? Watch then say. ▷

- a bike
- bags
- sun cream
- a rock pool
- shells
- a kite
- a sandcastle
- a bird
- a frisbee
- an ice cream

3 Think 💭 What are your answers to the Big Question?

Keep a list of your answers on the Big Question poster.

THE BIG QUESTION POSTER

UNIT 6 — What's a great day out?

OUR ANSWERS

4 Answer the Big Poll.

5 Watch the Big Question video again. ▷ Complete the activities. AB Page 60 ▷

Tess

1 **Think** 💭 What new activities would you like to do?

2 Listen, point and repeat. 🔊 098
Compare your list with Tess's.

3 Say which activities you can do in your area.

What's a great day out?
We can try a new activity.

Tess's list

1 go rafting

2 go to the theatre

3 watch a basketball match

4 go to a museum

5 visit an aquarium

6 visit a TV studio

7 see a parade

8 go to a funfair

9 visit a lighthouse

10 go bowling

4 Listen and sing. 🔊 099

Have you ever been to a funfair?
Yes, I have. The rides were cool!
Have you ever been to the theatre?
Yes, I have. I went with our school.

Have you ever seen a parade?
Yes, I have. There was one last year.
Have you ever visited a lighthouse?
No, I haven't. What a great idea!

Let's do something different!
Let's do something new!
Let's go and visit a lighthouse!
It's a fun thing to do!

Have you ever been rafting?
No, I haven't. I've never done that.
Have you ever been bowling?
No, I haven't. I've never done that.

Let's do something different!
Let's do something new!
Let's go rafting and bowling.
They're fun things to do!

5 **Communicate** 💬 Ask and answer. 🔊 100

Did you go rafting last summer?
No, I didn't.

Did you visit an aquarium last weekend?
Yes, I did!

1 **Listen, read and look at the picture.** 🔊 101

Who has seen the basketball player Giant Jim?

Hi Amelia! I'm watching a basketball match today. I'm with my sister. We're in the sports hall now.

Fantastic! Have you seen any famous players?

Yes, I have. I've seen Bob Birdman and Giant Jim, too! Look! This is Bob Birdman.

Lucky you! I've never been to a basketball match, but I've seen Giant Jim.

Really? Where did you see him?

I was at the theatre. He sat in front of me. It was impossible to see anything!

2 **Listen and follow.** 🔊 102 **Ask and answer about you.**

| Have you ever | watched a basketball match? |
| | been to the theatre? |

Yes, I have.	I	watched a match	yesterday.			
		went to the theatre	in	June.	the spring.	2016.
			last	weekend.	month.	winter.
No, I haven't.	I	've	never	watched a match.	been to the theatre.	

3 **Look, listen and read.** 🔊 103

Have you ever been to a funfair?

Yes, I have.

So you're Jake or Enzo. When did you go?

I went in 2016.

I know! You're Jake!

4 **Communicate** 💬 **Play the game.**

Jake — FUN FAIR CHILD 2016 / AQUARIUM CHILD 2017

Enzo — BOWLING ALLEY CHILD 2016 / FUN FAIR CHILD 2017

Alp — AQUARIUM CHILD 2016 / LIGHTHOUSE CHILD 2017

Adisa — LIGHTHOUSE CHILD 2016 / BOWLING ALLEY CHILD 2017

Ben

1 Think 💭 What attractions are there at a funfair?

2 Listen, point and repeat. 🔊 105

3 Which of these attractions have you been on? Which haven't you been on?

What's a great day out?
I love going to the funfair.

THE BiG Quest

Freddy's Funfair World

Ben's list

1 big wheel

2 roller coaster

3 bumper cars

4 merry-go-round

5 bungee trampoline

6 fun house

4 **BEFORE YOU READ** This is a story about a problem in Freddy's Funfair World. What do you think the problem is?

5 Listen, read and check your ideas. 🔊 106

6 **AFTER YOU READ** Watch the story video. ▷ Complete the activities. **AB Page 63**

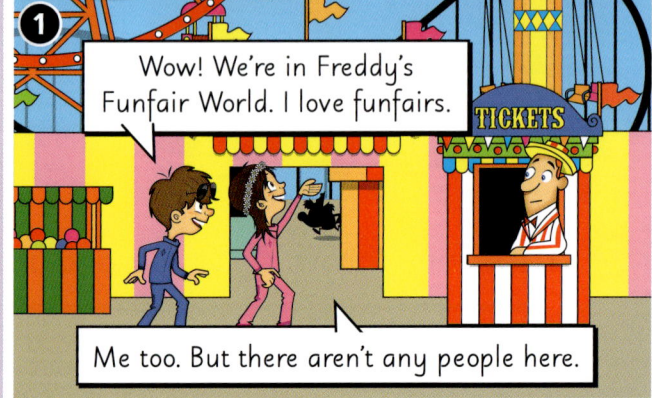

1 Wow! We're in Freddy's Funfair World. I love funfairs.

Me too. But there aren't any people here.

2 Hello! You're my first visitors today.

But why? It's a fantastic funfair.

A clown is playing tricks on the visitors. They don't like coming here now.

3 **Challenge**
Help Freddy stop the clown.
Win *free rides* all day!

Come on, Ben. We can do this!

But where is the clown?

1 REMEMBER THE STORY **Read and match.**

1 What about
2 Let's
3 Why don't we
4 How about

a starting the rain?
b follow him.
c using the bungee trampolines?
d start the moving floor?

Ben   Sophie

2 **Look at the verbs used in the suggestions from the story. Then say *a* or *b*.**

a *What about* and *How about*   b *Let's* and *Why don't we*
1 We use the infinitive after _____.
2 We use the *-ing* form of the verb after _____.

3 **Listen and follow.** 107 Think **Imagine you're at a funfair with a friend. Suggest what to do together.**

| Let's
Why don't we | go on | the bumper cars
the merry-go-round | ! |
| How about
What about | going on | the roller coaster
the big wheel | ? |

Look!

We agree with suggestions like this.
Good idea!   OK!   Great!
We disagree and make different suggestions like this.
I don't think so. Let's …
I'm not sure. Why don't we … ?

4 Think, pair, share! **Imagine you're at a friend's house. Suggest what to do together. Then tell your class.**

watch a DVD   make cupcakes   do a jigsaw
water the plants   play volleyball   hang out the clothes

We've decided to play cards.

Why don't we watch a DVD?

I'm not sure. How about playing cards?

OK. That's a good idea.

1 Look. How many things do you need to do the experiment? How many steps are there in the experiment?

What's a great day out?

Doing an experiment at the Science Museum is exciting.

Mason

Do a density experiment

You need

| a jar | vegetable oil | vinegar | food colouring | bicarbonate of soda |

1 Put 100 ml of vinegar into a jar or bottle.

2 Add ten drops of red food colouring.

3 Add 250 ml of vegetable oil.

The oil floats on the vinegar.

4 Add a spoon of bicarbonate of soda.

The vinegar and bicarbonate of soda make gas bubbles.

5 Observe the gas bubbles.

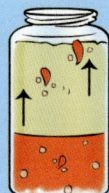

The gas bubbles carry the red vinegar to the top of the jar.

6 Observe the red vinegar.

The gas escapes at the top of the glass. Then the red vinegar sinks to the bottom of the jar again.

Why does the red vinegar go up and down?

10 ml of vinegar is heavier than 10 ml of oil.

Scientists say vinegar is denser than oil. That is why oil floats on vinegar.

Vinegar   Oil

Gas bubbles aren't as dense as vinegar or oil. They float to the top of the jar. They take the vinegar with them. When the gas escapes, the vinegar sinks because it's denser than the oil.

2 Read and listen. 🔊109 Then say.

1 Look at step 2. What colour is the vinegar?
2 Look at step 3. Which is on top: the oil or the vinegar?
3 Look at step 4. Where is the gas: in the oil or in the vinegar?
4 Look at step 5. Are the gas bubbles and the vinegar going up or down?
5 Look at step 6. Is the vinegar going up or down?
6 Which is the densest: oil, vinegar or gas?

3 **Think, pair, share!** Can you order these things from the densest to the least dense? How can you check your ideas?

water	vegetable oil
honey	washing-up liquid
chocolate sauce	

What's a great day out?

Going somewhere new is fun.

Alenka

1 **BEFORE YOU READ** Look at the photos. What are the adverts for?

2 **Think** What information do you need from an advert?

3 Read and listen. 🔊 111 Do these adverts give you the information you need?

Things to do in Croatia!

Go rafting on the Cetina River

The adventure starts when you put on your wetsuit, helmet and life jacket. When everybody is ready, the rafts can go!

In some places, the river is green and quiet. In other places, there's white water and the ride is exciting!

There's a break in the middle of the trip. You can have a snack, swim in the river near a small waterfall and dive off the high rocks into a deep, green pool.

It's a great day out! You'll love your rafting adventure!

Time: 3 hours
Prices: children under 16 – €15
        adults – €30
Includes: wetsuits, helmets and life jackets
For more information and booking, go to: www.cetinaadventures.hr

Have an underground adventure at Grabovača Cave Park!

There's a lot to do in the Grabovača Cave Park. Underground rivers formed some amazing caves here thousands of years ago. We offer guided tours of the Samograd Cave, the biggest cave in the park.

The guide will take you down the 470 steps into the cave. The cave is full of fantastic rock formations. There are beautiful green stalactites and stalagmites, and there are two bridges made of rock. It's a great experience!

Time: 1 hour

Prices: children under 16 – €5   adults – €6

Includes: guide

Important: Wear warm clothes and strong shoes

For more information and booking, go to: www.croatiaadventures.hr

4 **AFTER YOU READ**
Complete the activities. **AB Page 66**

Big Values!

Learn by trying new things.

1 Listen to Alenka talking to her grandma. 🔊 112 Answer.

Which three things did Alenka do in the park?

> visit the cave   go kayaking   go hiking   go on a bike ride

2 Listen again. 🔊 112 Are the sentences true or false? Say.

1 Alenka's grandma has never visited the Grabovača Cave Park.
2 Alenka liked the white rocks in the cave best.
3 Alenka learned about some rare flowers.
4 There are bears in the park.
5 After lunch, everybody went kayaking.
6 Alenka doesn't like kayaking.

3 **Think, pair, share!** What natural spaces are there in your area?

4 Complete the activities. **AB Page 67** ▶

Lesson 9 Writing **The Big Write AB Pages 68–69**

Lesson 10 **THE BIG QUESTION REVIEW**

REVIEW VIDEO

1 Watch and answer the questions on the review video. ▶

2 Look back at the unit and say the missing words.
Then compare your answers on the Big Question poster.

A trip to the ▢ is great.

Doing an experiment at the Science ▢ is exciting.

We can try a new ▢ .

Going somewhere ▢ is fun.

I love going to the ▢ .

I like showing someone else my ▢ places.

3 **Communicate** 💬 Ask and answer.

4 Complete the self-evaluation activities. **AB Page 69** ▶

Which is your favourite answer?

'I love going to the funfair.' My friends like it, too!

1 Read and circle the correct words.

Yasmina: Have you ever ¹ (saw) (seen) a parade?

Leon: Yes, I ² (have) (did). I ³ (saw) (have seen) a parade last year in London.

Yasmina: That sounds good! I ⁴ (have) (did) never ⁵ (saw) (seen) a parade.

Leon: ⁶ (Have) (Has) you ever ⁷ (visited) (visit) an aquarium?

Yasmina: Yes, I ⁸ (did) (have). I ⁹ (visited) (have visited) an aquarium with my family last summer.

Leon: ¹⁰ (Have) (Did) you like it?

Yasmina: Yes, I ¹¹ (have) (did)! The penguins were really cool!

2 Think 💭 Write the questions. Write short answers for you.

visit

see

watch

go

Question

1 *Have you ever visited a castle?* _____

_____

2 _____

_____

3 _____

_____

4 _____

_____

3 Communicate 💬 Ask your partner the questions from activity 2. Write your partner's answers. 📝

Have you ever visited a castle?

Yes, I have. I went last month.

4 Write about yourself and your partner. 📝

We've both visited a castle. I went last year and James went last month.

5 Read and match.

1 How   a play cards.
2 Why   b about playing volleyball?
3 What   c about going in the fun house?
4 Let's   d don't we go on the bumper cars?

6 Complete the conversations.

| do | don't | ~~go~~ | going | ~~good~~ | great | sure | watching |

1 Let's _____*go*_____ on the roller coaster!
_____*Good*_____ idea!

2 How about _____ on the merry-go-round?
I'm not _____.

3 Why don't we _____ a jigsaw?
Yes! _____!

4 What about _____ a DVD?
I _____ think so. I'm tired.

7 Choose four things that you'd like to do this weekend with a friend. Write suggestions.

Let's	go / bowling	play / basketball
What about	go to / the zoo	play / video games
Why don't we	do / a jigsaw	go to / the park
How about	read / comics	go / swimming

What about reading comics? _____

_____

_____

_____

8 Communicate 💬 Work in pairs. Take turns to make suggestions. Find two things you'd both like to do.

1 **BEFORE YOU READ** Look at the pictures.

    1 What differences are there between the first and the last picture?

    2 Which weather words do you think are in the fable?

2 Read and listen. 🔊 114 Check your answers.

3 **AFTER YOU READ** Ask and answer about the wind, the sun and the man.

> What did the wind do?

> It blew the snow off the fields.

4 Complete the activities. **AB Page 70**

THE SUN AND THE WIND

It was a beautiful winter's day. The fields were white with snow. The birds were in their nests and the rabbits were in their rabbit holes. There was ice on the river and on the puddles on the path. A man came along the path. He had a big jacket and a hat and a scarf.

The wind and the sun were in the sky. The wind said to the sun, 'I'm very strong! I can make kites fly. I can turn the sails of windmills. I blow sailing boats along the sea. I'm stronger than you.'

'Oh no, you aren't,' said the sun. 'I'm stronger than you.'

The wind laughed. 'I don't think so,' he said. 'I can blow down trees and houses. I can make storms at sea, and blow cows out of the fields.'

The sun listened quietly and smiled.

'What can you do?' asked the wind. 'Show me!'

The sun looked down at the Earth and had an idea.

'OK,' said the sun. 'Let's do an experiment.'

'An experiment!' said the wind. 'What experiment?'

'Can you see that man on the path?' asked the sun.

'Yes, I can,' said the wind. 'I'll blow him into the river!'

'No,' said the sun. 'Poor man. That isn't a good idea. Here's the experiment. Can you take off his jacket and scarf?'

'OK,' said the wind. 'That's easy. Watch.'

1 **Think** 💭 **Read the fable again. Answer the questions.**

   1 Who's stronger, the gentle sun or the violent wind?

   2 What's the message of the fable?

2 **Think, pair, share!** **Do you know any other fables? What's the message in them?**

3 **Complete the activities.** **AB Page 71**

The sun disappeared behind a cloud and watched. The wind started to blow hard.

He blew some branches off the trees. The man's hat flew off, too. 'Good!' thought the wind, 'I'm going to win!'

The wind blew some more. He blew the birds out of the trees. The man's scarf nearly flew away. 'Great!' thought the wind, 'But I have to blow harder.'

Now the wind blew as hard as he could. The man felt very cold. He tied his scarf more tightly around his neck and held onto his jacket.

'Hmm,' said the wind to the sun. 'Perhaps it isn't as easy as I thought. It's your turn now. I can't blow any more.'

The sun started to shine gently. The snow disappeared from the fields. The ice disappeared from the river. The sun shone more strongly. The birds started to sing. The rabbits came out of their holes and played in the fields. The man stopped and looked around. 'What a beautiful day it is now!' he said. 'I'm hot. I'm going to sit down where it's cool.' He took off his scarf and his jacket and he sat under a tree by the path.

'You see,' said the sun to the wind, 'I'm stronger than you.'

Create a book character

1 **Think** 💭 Number the project stages in order in your notebook. 📘
Then look at pages 88–91 and check. **WHOLE CLASS**

a Find out which characters your group likes.

b Think about your favourite book characters.

c Plan what you're going to say in your presentation.

d Choose which character your group wants to create.

e Present your character to your class.

f Make your book character.

Think about it

2 **Think** 💭 Answer the questions. **WHOLE CLASS**

1 What are your three favourite books?
2 Who are the main characters in your favourite books?
3 Who's your favourite character? Why do you like him / her?

3 **Communicate** 💬 Look at the pictures and answer. **PROJECT GROUP**

Willy Wonka   **Bilbo Baggins**   **The Red Queen**   **Cinderella**

1 Which books are the characters from?

Alice in Wonderland   Charlie and the Chocolate Factory   Cinderella   The Hobbit

2 Match an adjective to each character.

bad   beautiful   brave   clever

3 What does each character usually wear? Does he / she often carry something?
4 Do you know the most important thing each character does in his / her story?

4 Discuss the books you like and choose one book for your project. Then make four lists of characters. **PROJECT GROUP**

- the main boy characters
- the main adult characters
- the main girl characters
- any other interesting characters

5 Find out about favourite book characters in your group. Make notes in your Activity Book. **AB Page 72 Activities 1–2** **PROJECT GROUP**

Pupil 1 Which boy character from your book does your group like?

Pupil 2 Which girl character from your book does your group like?

Pupil 3 Which adult character from your book does your group like?

Pupil 4 Which other character from your book does your group like?

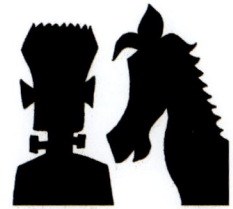

Choose

6 **Collaborate** Tell your group your information. Choose one character to create. **AB Page 72 Activity 3** **PROJECT GROUP**

Three of us would like to create Alice.

One of us wants to create the Cat.

Two of us think creating the Red Queen would be fun.

Let's create Alice. She's brave, pretty and clever.

Plan

7 Look, listen and match. Then listen and repeat. 🔊 115 WHOLE CLASS

1 Why don't we show Alice at the tea party?

OK. Shall we make her look surprised?

2 Let's make her hair from yellow wool!

That's a good idea.

3 We can make her dress from a blue T-shirt.

Great!

4 How about giving her a toy white rabbit?

I'm not sure. What about giving her a tea cup?

English in use

Remember to use *Let's … !, How about … ?, What about … ?* and *Why don't we … ?* to make suggestions.

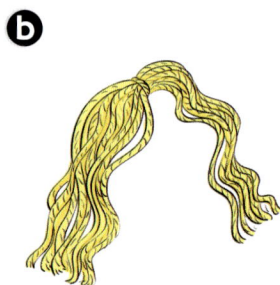

a

b

c

d

8 Decide which scene you want to show your book character in, and what he / she is going to look like. Think about his / her clothes, hair and accessories. How are you going to make them? AB Page 73 Activity 4 PROJECT GROUP

Make

9 Create 💡 Choose jobs. Make your book character. PROJECT GROUP

Step 1
Decide who is going to make the character's head and body.

Step 2
Decide who is going to make the character's clothes and where you can find the accessories.

Step 3
Decide who's going to present your character to the class and what you will say about him / her.

Alice
Young girl - main character in Alice in Wonderland.

This scene - Alice is at a strange tea party

10 Present your book character to your class. Then answer questions from your class. WHOLE CLASS

> This is Alice from *Alice in Wonderland*. We all like this character.

> She looks surprised because in this scene she's at a strange tea party.

> How did you make her?

> Her cup is from my little sister's tea set.

> My mum gave us some yellow wool for her hair.

11 Match the questions to the answers. WHOLE CLASS

1 What did you enjoy about this project?
2 What did you find difficult?
3 Were you surprised by anything?
4 How could you do the project better next time?

a We should make sure we can find clothes for the character at home.

c I liked choosing the clothes for our character.

b The head was difficult to make.

d There are a lot of characters in *Alice in Wonderland*. That surprised me!

12 Now answer the questions for your project. Use your answers to write a summary. PROJECT GROUP

Charlie's star post ⭐

I felt bad when I got lost.

Sing along with Ben

Look with Tess

Puzzle World

Charlie and the chocolate factory
Roald Dahl

Find out with Lily

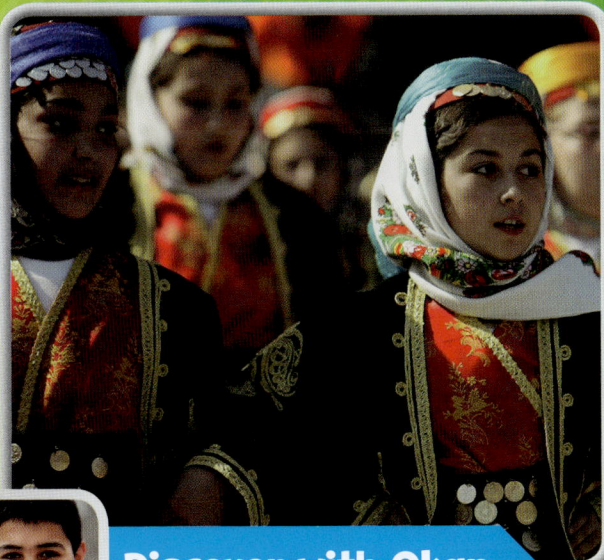

Discover with Okan

BIG POLL

Do you feel better ...

in the mornings

or

in the afternoons?

1 Look and answer.

1 What's the Big Question for unit 7?
2 Who are the posts from?
3 What can you see in the pictures?

2 Which things do you see in the Big Question video? Watch then say. ▷

- a train
- a motorbike
- a bus
- a plane
- Buckingham Palace
- the Queen
- a cinema
- a café
- a cook
- a police officer

3 Think 💭 What are your answers to the Big Question?

Keep a list of your answers on the Big Question poster.

UNIT **7**   THE BIG QUESTION POSTER

What makes us feel good or bad?

OUR ANSWERS

4 Answer the Big Poll.

5 Watch the Big Question video again. ▷ Complete the activities. **AB Page 74** ▶

7 Lesson 2 Vocabulary and song

Ben

What makes us feel good or bad?

I feel bad when I'm poorly.

1 **Think** What health problems do people sometimes have?

2 Listen, point and repeat. 🔊117 Compare your list with Ben's.

3 Say which of these health problems you had last winter.

Ben's list

 **1** a cold

 **2** a cough

 **3** a stomach-ache

 **4** a headache

 **5** toothache

 **6** a sore throat

 **7** a temperature

 **8** earache

 **9** a pain in my chest

 **10** backache

4 Listen and sing. 🔊118

Monday morning. I'm here at school.
I'm fed up. There's nobody here!
They're all at home. They're all in bed.
They're all very poorly. Oh dear, oh dear!

A cough, a sniff, an ouch, atchoo!
Everybody's poorly. Get better soon!

Jane has had earache for two days now.
Tom has got toothache. It won't go away.
They're all at home. They're all in bed.
They're all very poorly, but I want to play!

Chorus

Ray has got a terrible pain in his chest.
Flo has had a cold since last weekend.
They're all at home. They're all in bed.
Everybody's poorly! I want my friends!

Chorus

Bill has got a temperature –
  it's very high.
He's had backache since Sunday, too.
They're all at home. They're all in bed.
Please, everybody, get better soon!

Chorus

5 **Communicate** Ask and answer. 🔊119

Which makes you feel worse, a cough or a headache?

A headache. What about you?

A cough makes me feel worse.

1 Listen, read and look at the picture. 🔊 120

What's the matter with Charlie?

Hi Charlie! Where are you?
You've been off school for three days!

Look at my photo! I'm at home.
I'm not feeling well. 🙁

Oh no! What's the matter?

I've had a temperature since Monday.
And I've had a cold for two days.

That's terrible. Are you feeling better now?

Yes, I'm going to go to school tomorrow.
By the way, was the maths test difficult?

The teacher changed the day. It's tomorrow.

Oh! I think I've got a stomach-ache now!

2 Listen and follow. 🔊 121 **Think** 💭 Say true sentences about Charlie.

| I | 've | had | a cold
a cough
a temperature
a headache
a stomach-ache
a sore throat | for | one day. two days.
a week. three weeks.
a month. six months. |
| He
She | 's | | | since | yesterday. Monday.
last week. my birthday.
last month. January. |

3 Look, listen and read. 🔊 122

She's had a temperature for three days.

Ana or Deka! Go on.

She's had a headache since Wednesday.

I know! It's Deka.

4 **Communicate** 💬 Play the game.

	Wednesday	Thursday	Today (Friday)
Ana			
Lina			
Fen			
Deka			

Tess

1 **Think** 💭 What makes you feel good?

2 Listen, point and repeat. 🔊 124

3 Which of these have you done?
Which haven't you done?

What makes us feel good or bad?

I feel good when I can solve a puzzle.

THE BiG Quest **Puzzle World**

Tess's list

1 run 5 kilometres

2 win a cup

3 solve a puzzle

4 make a new friend

5 have a good idea

6 pass my piano exam

① **Challenge**
Read the clues, find the letters and make the word. Then find the prize. You've got **5 minutes**!

Clue 1 Clue 2 Clue 3

We're in Puzzle World. Look!

② A race against time! Quick! Read the first clue.

My first letter is in the living room.

4 **BEFORE YOU READ** This story is in Puzzle World. What puzzles do you think Tess and Noah will find?

5 Listen, read and check your ideas. 🔊 125

6 **AFTER YOU READ** Watch the story video. ▷
Complete the activities. **AB Page 77**

③ We're in the living room.

But there aren't any letters here.

4 I've just had a good idea. What is there in the picture?

A boat on the sea. 'Sea' … C … the first letter is C.

5 Quick! Open the second clue.

My second letter is in the bedroom. It's in the musical instruments.

6 There isn't anything in the flute.

Look! There's an S in the drum. But … wait a minute …

7 I knew it! Trick!

8 Why are you smiling?

Trick has just solved the clue. Look at the letters! There's a U in 'drum' and in 'flute'. The second letter is U.

9 Quick! Read the last clue.

My third letter is in the kitchen. It's a green vegetable.

10 A green vegetable. Lettuce, spinach, peas, …

'Pea' – P! The third letter is P!

11 C–U–P spells 'cup'.

There's a cup in the hall. Let's go!

We've just won the cup!

LEVEL UP >>>

Tess   Noah

1 **REMEMBER THE STORY** Read. Which sentence isn't in the story? Say.

1 I've just had a good idea.
2 Trick has just solved the clue.
3 They've just passed an exam.
4 We've just won the cup!

2 Look at the position of *just* in the sentences in activity 1. Choose.

Which sentence is correct?
a I've just solved a puzzle.
b Just I've solved a puzzle.

3 Listen and follow. 🔊 126 **Think** 💭 Mime. Say what has just happened.

I We They	've		had a good idea. solved a puzzle. won a cup. passed a piano exam. run 5 kilometres. made a new friend.
		just	
He She	's		

Look!

We use *just* to talk about something which happened a very short time ago.
Why are you tired?
I've just run 5 kilometres.

4 **Think, pair, share!** Imagine a situation and choose an adjective for how you feel. Say what you've just done.

| happy   cold   tired   bad |

| made a snowman   helped a friend   had a PE lesson |
| run for the bus   eaten a lot   said the wrong answer |

I feel cold.

Why?

I've just made a snowman.

She feels cold because she's just made a snowman.

What makes us feel good or bad?

I feel good when I read a good book.

Lily

1 Look. What is the story wheel about?

2 Look and read. How many steps are there to make a story wheel?

My story wheel

Do you know the book *Charlie and the Chocolate Factory* by Roald Dahl? It's a great book. This is my story wheel for the book. I made it like this.

1 I made a list of the most important scenes in the book. Then I chose eight. I drew a picture for each scene in the segments of the story wheel.

2 I cut out the window in the cover, and then I wrote the title and the author's name.

3 I put the story wheel together with a split pin.

3 Match the sentences to the segments.

a Charlie buys a chocolate bar and finds a golden ticket.
b Charlie and his family are poor. They live next to the chocolate factory.
c Mike Teavee wants to get into the television, and shrinks.
d The factory is Willy Wonka's. He invents a competition. The five winners have to find a golden ticket in their chocolate bar. The prize is a visit to the chocolate factory.
e Veruca Salt takes a squirrel and then falls into the rubbish.
f Charlie doesn't break the rules, and Willy Wonka gives him the factory.
g In the factory, Augustus Gloop falls into the chocolate river.
h Violet Beauregarde eats some chewing gum and changes into a berry.

4 Think, pair, share! How do the children in these scenes feel?

1 BEFORE YOU READ Look at the photos. What did class 5B do in the show?

What makes us feel good or bad?
Doing a school show makes me feel good.

Okan

2 Think How did the children feel before, during and after their performances?

3 Read and listen. 129 Were your ideas about their feelings correct?

5B's class blog

Home   About   Photo gallery   Popular post   Archive

Year 5 show   5th April   3 comments

We've just had our school show! We had a great time. We all felt really good after the performance. Here are some photos and some blog posts from Class 5B. We'd love to read your comments!   *Adnan İpek*

We danced the *Kaşık Oyunu*. *Kaşık Oyunu* means the Spoon Dance. We had two wooden spoons in each hand. We clicked the spoons while we danced, and we wore traditional costumes. Before the dance, we were nervous because it's a difficult dance. But I think we danced it well. My favourite part was clicking the spoons.

Eda

We sang a song in English. It's called *Yellow Submarine* and it's by The Beatles. They were a famous British pop group. I like the song a lot because it's funny. It makes me feel happy when I sing it. It's about some people who live in a yellow submarine! Everybody liked it. The audience sang with us!

Yasemin

PROGRAMME

This is the programme for our play. It's a story by Nasreddin Hodja, a famous Turkish man who lived about 800 years ago. He was a wise man and he told funny stories. Our play is about a man and a boy walking to market with their donkey. In the end, the man and the boy carry the donkey! We had to wear special costumes, and we had to remember a lot of words. We were tired at the end of the play.

Yusuf

4 AFTER YOU READ
Complete the activities.   AB Page 80

Big Values!

It's fine to feel nervous before an important event.

7 **Lesson 8** Culture

1 **Listen to Okan.** 🔊 130 **Answer.**

What did Okan do in the show?

| dance   sing the song   act in the play |

2 **Listen again.** 🔊 130 **Read the sentences and say *a* or *b*.**

1 Okan … good at dancing.   **a** is   **b** isn't
2 The song … easy to learn.   **a** was   **b** wasn't
3 They painted the submarine … .   **a** yellow   **b** blue
4 Okan … nervous before the play.   **a** was   **b** wasn't
5 Yusuf … the part of Nasreddin Hodja.   **a** played   **b** didn't play
6 Okan's grandma … the play.   **a** watched   **b** didn't watch

3 **Think, pair, share!** Have you taken part in a school show? How did you feel?

4 **Complete the activities.** AB Page 81

Lesson 9 Writing The **Big Write** AB Pages 82–83

Lesson 10 THE BIG QUESTION REVIEW

1 Watch and answer the questions on the review video. ▷

REVIEW VIDEO

2 Look back at the unit and say the missing words.
Then compare your answers on the Big Question poster.

I felt bad when I got ▭ .

I feel good when I ▭ a good book.

I feel bad when I'm ▭ .

Doing a school ▭ makes me feel good.

I feel good when I can ▭ a puzzle.

I feel bad when I can't play ▭ .

3 **Communicate** 💬 Ask and answer.

Which is your favourite answer?

'Doing a school show makes me feel good.' I read a poem at our school show.

4 **Complete the self-evaluation activities.** AB Page 83

1 Read and write *True* or *False*. Correct the false sentences.

Sun   Thurs

1 I've had a headache for five days.   *True*

_____

Wed   Fri

2 Jane's had a stomach-ache since yesterday. _____

_____

1st Jan   1st Feb

3 Jamie's had a cough for two months. _____

_____

Tues   Tues

4 I've had earache since last week. _____

_____

2 Read and complete with *for* or *since*.

1 (My friend) (a cold) (a week.)   *My friend has had a cold for a week.*

2 (My teacher) (backache) (Tuesday.) _____

3 (I) (a sore throat) (two days.) _____

4 (My cousins) (toothache) (last week.) _____

5 (My uncle) (a sore throat) (five days.) _____

6 (My mum) (a pain in her chest) (this morning.) _____

3 Write sentences like the ones in activity 2 about some of your family and friends.

My mum has had a headache since last night.

1 _____

2 _____

4 **Read and match.**

1 I feel tired.

2 I feel happy.

3 I feel cold.

4 I feel sad.

a I've just lost my watch.

b I've just made a snowman.

c I've just run 5 kilometres.

d I've just passed my piano exam.

5 **Look and write.**

| win a competition   pass an exam   solve a puzzle   ~~win a race~~ |

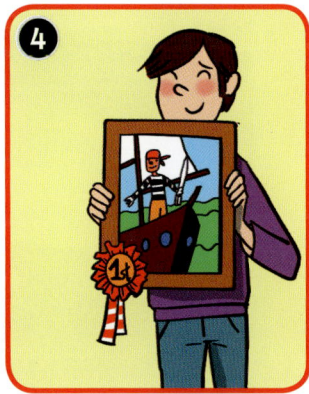

1 Leila _has just won a race._

2 Karim _____

3 Maya _____

4 Youssef _____

6 **Think** 💭 **Imagine three things that you've just done. Write sentences.**

I feel tired. I've just _____

I feel happy. _____

I feel _____

7 **Communicate** 💬 **Tell your partner about your answers to activity 6.**

8 Where do people work?

Poppy's star post ⭐

It's nice to work at home.

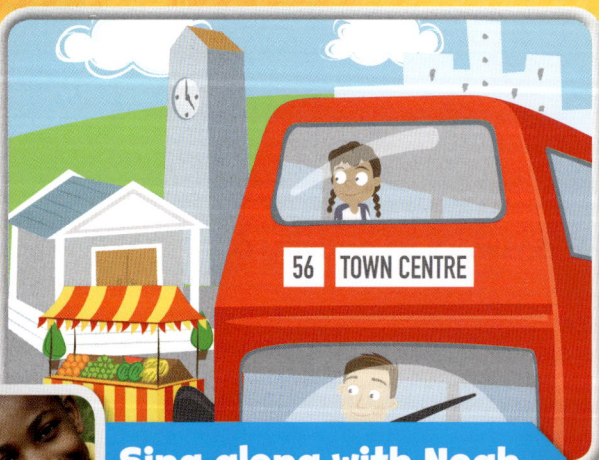

Sing along with Noah

Look with Sophie

Film World

Find out with Tess

Discover with Fabio

BIG POLL
Would you prefer to work ... with people or with machines?

1 Look and answer.

1 What's the Big Question for unit 8?
2 Who are the posts from?
3 What can you see in the pictures?

2 Which things do you see in the Big Question video? Watch then say. ▷

- a factory
- a shop
- a garden
- a bookcase
- a laptop
- glasses
- a cushion
- paper
- pens
- a television

3 Think 💭 What are your answers to the Big Question?

Keep a list of your answers on the Big Question poster.

UNIT 8 THE BIG QUESTION POSTER
Where do people work?

OUR ANSWERS

4 Answer the Big Poll.

5 Watch the Big Question video again. ▷ Complete the activities. AB Page 84 ▷

Noah

1 Think 💭 Where do your family and friends work?

2 Listen, point and repeat. 🔊 133
Compare your list with Noah's.

3 Say which of these places is or isn't in your town.

Where do people work?

We can help others by working in a hospital.

Noah's list

1 sports centre

2 tourist office

3 supermarket

4 town hall

5 market

6 university

7 bus station

8 fire station

9 bank

10 post office

4 Listen and sing. 🔊 134

Welcome to my town –
An important place to me!
Let's get a bus from the bus station
And see what we can see!

This is the tourist office
Where Mum works at weekends.
This is our sports centre
Where I swim with my friends.

Chorus

This is the place where Dad works.
It's our town hall.
This is the market
Where my uncle has a stall.

Chorus

This is the supermarket
Where we buy our food.
Can you see the bank,
And the post office, too?

Chorus

This is our hospital –
An important place for us all!
It's a very special place for me:
It's the place where I was born!

5 Communicate 💬 Ask and answer. 🔊 135

Have you ever been to a tourist office?

No, I haven't.

Have you ever been to a sports centre?

Yes, I have.

1 **Listen, read and look at the picture.** 🔊 136

Where is Noah?

Hi Poppy! Look at this photo! Guess where I am!

No idea. It's a terrible photo. Give me a clue.

It's the place where my uncle works now. He's got a new job.

OK. What does he do?

He's the person who brings your food.

I know! Your uncle is a waiter and you're at a restaurant. Lucky you!

2 **Listen and follow.** 🔊 137 **Make a sentence about a place and a person for your partner to guess.**

It's the place	where	my uncle works.	we take the bus.
		people get money.	people buy food.
		I play football.	people get married.

| He's She's | the person who | brings your food. | works at the fire station. |
| | | looks after the animals. | makes people better. |

3 **Look, listen and read.** 🔊 138

She's the person who looks after the animals.

I know! That's the zoo keeper. A2.

That's right. Your turn.

It's the place where people buy food.

4 **Communicate** 💬 **Play the game.**

	A	B	C
1			
2			
3			

1   **Think** 💭 Who works in a film or TV studio?

2   Listen, point and repeat. 🔊 140

3   Which job would you like to do?
Which wouldn't you like to do?

Where do people work?   **Sophie**

Working in a film studio is exciting.

Sophie's list

1 stunt person

2 actor

3 wardrobe assistant

4 make-up artist

5 director

6 cameraman

4   **BEFORE YOU READ** This story is about a visit to a film studio. Can you guess who the children meet?

5   Listen, read and check your ideas. 🔊 141

6   **AFTER YOU READ** Watch the story video. ▷ Complete the activities. **AB Page 87**

THE BiG Quest — Film World

1

Challenge
What film are they making?
Win a *video camera*!

Look, Sophie. We're in a film studio in Film World. And here's the challenge.

Cool. Let's ask that man.

2

Excuse me. What were you doing?

I was filming the actors. I'm the cameraman.

3

Oh good. What film is this?

Lights! Camera! Action!

Shh. You mustn't talk now. We're filming.

1 **REMEMBER THE STORY** Read.
Which sentence isn't in the story? Say.

1 I was filming the actors.
2 What were you doing?
3 I was looking after the costumes.
4 I was telling everybody what to do.

 Sophie
 Mason

2 **Look at the sentences from the story. Read and choose.**

1 The sentences are about	**a** the present.	**b** the past.
2 The sentences use *was* or *were* +	**a** verb + *-ing*.	**b** verb + *-ed*.
3 The sentences are about	**a** a single action.	**b** a continuous action.

3 **Listen and follow.** 🔊 142 **Think** 💭 **Make sentences.**

What were you doing	at ten o'clock at half past two	yesterday? on Monday?
I was	filming the actors. doing stunts. doing the make-up. looking after the costumes. playing the hero. telling everybody what to do.	

Look!

We use *was* + verb + *-ing* to talk about a continuous action in the past.

4 **Think, pair, share!** **Think about what you were doing at these times yesterday. Ask and answer.**

having breakfast
getting dressed
watching TV
doing maths
going home
playing football

What were you doing at seven o'clock yesterday?

I was getting dressed.

1 Look. What are people making in the photos?

2 Read and find seven jobs.

Where do people work?
Some people work on farms.

Tess

1 Coffee is made from the fruit of the coffee tree. The fruit is called coffee cherries. Coffee trees grow on farms.

2 Farmers and their families pick the cherries when they're ready.

3 This is the machine which takes the coffee beans out of the cherries.

4 The farmer dries the beans in the sun.

5 Farm workers sort the beans into different sizes.

6 This is a coffee taster who tries the beans and decides if they make good coffee.

7 Sailors take the coffee beans all over the world on big ships.

8 Factory workers roast the beans in machines at 200°C.

9 This is one of the lorry drivers who takes the coffee to the shops.

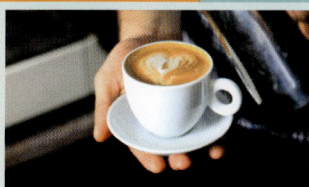

10 Waiters in coffee shops work hard to make a great cup of coffee for their customers.

3 Find and say one extra sentence for each photo.

a They take two to six weeks to dry.
b They take it to restaurants and cafés, too.
c Then the beans go from the ship to the factory.
d There are a lot of different types of coffee to choose from.
e The trees grow in hot countries, like Ghana, where there's a lot of rain.
f There are ten different sizes of beans.
g A coffee taster tastes hundreds of cups of coffee every day.
h The cherries are red when they're ready to pick.
i There are two coffee beans in every cherry.
j The beans are brown after roasting.

4 **Think, pair, share!** Think about another food. Make a list of the people who help to make it.

Where do people work?

Working in an ice cream shop is cool!

Fabio

1 BEFORE YOU READ Look at the photos. What is the article about?

2 Think 💭 Think of three questions to ask the ice cream maker.

3 Read and listen. 🔊 145 Did the article answer your questions?

A day in the life of an Italian ice cream maker

Gelato means *ice cream* in Italian. And Italian *gelaterías*, or ice cream shops, are famous all over the world. We all love ice cream, but have you thought about the people behind the counter? Find out about Luciano Ricci and his job in his Italian ice cream shop.

6.00 am Luciano is at the market. He's buying fruit to make his ice cream. He buys different fruit in different seasons: lemons in spring; strawberries, melons and peaches in summer; pears and grapes in autumn; oranges in winter. Luciano always uses natural ingredients in his ice creams.

7.00 am Luciano arrives at his shop. He turns on his favourite music and he starts making ice cream. He sells 30 different flavours in his shop. Some are traditional, like chocolate or vanilla, but he also makes unusual flavours, like rose. 'My ice creams are very special,' says Luciano. 'I love inventing new flavours.'

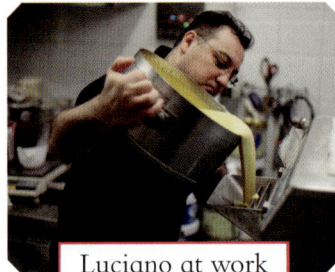

Luciano at work

9.30 am All the ice creams are ready and in their boxes. Before they go to the counter, Luciano decorates them with chocolate, fruit, nuts and flowers.

A lot of flavours to choose from!

10.00 am The shop opens. Luciano's sister and his mum arrive and help in the shop. Soon there's a queue of people. Italians eat ice cream all year. A favourite Italian breakfast is cake and ice cream!

Help from the family

12.00 pm Now the shop is really busy. 'Lots of people have ice cream for lunch,' says Luciano. 'It's fast, delicious and natural. Perfect for a sunny day!'

6.00 pm The shop closes. Luciano and his family tidy up. It's time to go home.

4 AFTER YOU READ
Complete the activities. **AB Page 90**

Big Values!
Be proud of your work.

1 Listen to Fabio. 🔊 146 Answer.

Which members of his family does Fabio talk about?

| dad | mum | sister | brother | grandma | grandpa |

2 Listen again. 🔊 146 Answer the questions. 📝

1 Does Fabio ever work in the ice cream shop?
2 Is popcorn ice cream Fabio's favourite flavour?
3 Does Fabio's mum like ice cream?
4 Does Fabio's mum make birthday cakes?
5 Is Fabio's sister a waiter?
6 Is Fabio's dad good at cleaning the kitchen?

3 **Think, pair, share!** What jobs do people in your family do?

4 Complete the activities. **AB Page 91**

Lesson **9** Writing The **Big Write** AB Pages 92–93

Lesson **10**   **THE BIG QUESTION REVIEW**

1 Watch and answer the questions on the review video. ▶

REVIEW VIDEO

2 Look back at the unit and say the missing words.
Then compare your answers on the Big Question poster.

It's nice to work at ▢ .

Some people work on ▢ .

We can help others by working in a ▢ .

Working in an ▢ shop is cool!

Working in a ▢ is exciting.

Some people work in ▢ places.

3 **Communicate** 💬 Ask and answer.

Which is your favourite answer?

'Working in a film studio is exciting.' I'd like to be a make-up artist.

4 Complete the self-evaluation activities. **AB Page 93**

1 Read and circle the correct words. Number the pictures.

ⓐ ☐

ⓑ ☐

ⓒ 1

ⓓ ☐

ⓔ ☐

ⓕ ☐

1 He's the person (where) (**who**) cooks our food.

2 It's the place (**where**) (who) people buy food.

3 He's the person (where) (**who**) works at the fire station.

4 She's the person (where) (**who**) looks after the animals.

5 It's the place (**where**) (who) we take the bus.

6 She's the person (where) (**who**) makes people better.

2 Think 💭 Write about three places and three people in your town.

Places

1 *It's the place where* _____

2 _____

3 _____

People

1 _____ *the person who* _____

2 _____

3 _____

3 Communicate 💬 Tell your partner your sentences from activity 2. They guess the people and places.

< It's the place where I go swimming. >   < It's the swimming pool! >

4 Complete the conversations.

look after   fly   tell   film

What were you doing at nine o'clock this morning?

1 Wardrobe assistant: I _____*was looking after*_____ the costumes.

2 Director: I _____ people what to do.

3 Cameraman: I _____ the actors.

4 Stunt person: I _____!

5 Complete the questions and write the answers.

go to school   have lunch   play basketball   sleep

1 What were you doing at five o'clock yesterday morning?
  *I was sleeping.*_____

2 What were you _____ at eight o'clock yesterday morning?
_____

3 What _____ at half past twelve yesterday afternoon?
_____

4 _____ at four o'clock yesterday afternoon?
_____

5.00 am    8.00 am

12.30 pm    4.00 pm

6 **Communicate** 💬 Ask and answer the questions from activity 5. Use the times in the box.

6.00 am   10.00 am
1.00 pm   6.00 pm

What were you doing at six o'clock yesterday morning?

I was sleeping.

9 Where can we go shopping?

Eve's star post ⭐

Shopping in charity shops helps others.

Sing along with Dev

Look with Ania

one hundred and sixteen 116

Supermarket World

Find out with Sophie

Discover with Rosa

BIG POLL
Do you prefer shopping ...
in a shopping centre
or
in small shops?

1 Look and answer.

1 What's the Big Question for unit 9?
2 Who are the posts from?
3 What can you see in the pictures?

2 Which things do you see in the Big Question video? Watch then say. ▷

- books
- jigsaws
- dresses
- shoes
- necklaces
- DVDs
- board games
- cards
- dolls
- CDs

3 Think 💭 What are your answers to the Big Question?

Keep a list of your answers on the Big Question poster.

> UNIT 9
> THE BIG QUESTION POSTER
> Where can we go shopping?
> OUR ANSWERS

4 Answer the Big Poll.

5 Watch the Big Question video again. ▷ Complete the activities. **AB Page 94** ▷

1 Think 💭 What different kinds of shops are there?

2 Listen, point and repeat. 🔊 150
Compare your list with Dev's.

3 Say which of these places is or isn't in your area.

Where can we go shopping?

There are a lot of shops on the High Street.

Dev

Dev's list

1 baker's

2 chemist's

3 travel agent's

4 greengrocer's

5 bookshop

6 sports shop

7 toy shop

8 newsagent's

9 florist's

10 department store

4 Listen and sing. 🔊 151

Up and down the High Street
I've got a list from Mum
She's busy but she told me
That shopping can be fun.

I went into the baker's
I was looking for some bread
But the cakes were delicious
So I bought a few instead.

Chorus

I went into the newsagent's
I was standing in a queue
I saw some funny comics
So I bought just one or two.

Chorus

I went into the sports shop
I was looking for a ball
I found three that I liked
And so I bought them all.

And then I went back home
And took the things I bought
  to Mum
She wasn't very happy
But I think shopping's fun!

MAGAZINES

comic

5 Communicate 💬 Say and answer. 🔊 152

It's a place where you can buy bread.

A baker's.

It's a place where you can find unusual books.

A bookshop.

1 **Listen, read and look at the picture.** 🔊 153

What was Dev doing yesterday afternoon?

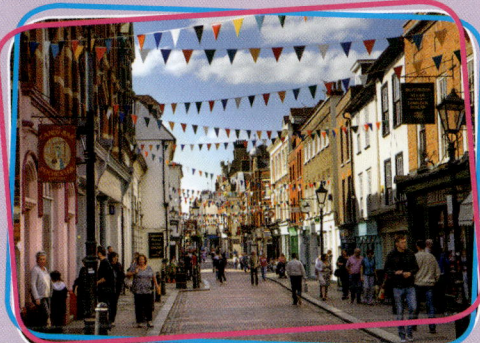

Hi Eve! Look at this photo of my high street.

That's pretty. When did you take it?

Yesterday. I was shopping with my mum all afternoon!

Did you buy anything?

Yes, I did. I bought an ice cream at the newsagent's. I was really hungry after all that shopping!

2 **Listen and follow.** 🔊 154 **Say where you were shopping and what you bought.**

What were you doing?	I was shopping at the	department store. toy shop. sports shop.
Did you buy anything?	Yes, I did. I bought	a T-shirt. a toy car. a football.
	No, I didn't.	

3 **Look, listen and read.** 🔊 155

I was shopping at the baker's.

Did you buy anything?

Yes, I did. I bought a cake.

I know! You're B.

4 **Communicate** 💬 **Play the game.**

A B C D E F

1 **Think** 💭 What can you buy in a supermarket?

2 Listen, point and repeat. 🔊 157

3 What other food can you often find in these containers?

Where can we go shopping?

I like buying my favourite food at the supermarket.

Ania

Ania's list

1 a bottle of water

2 a tin of tuna

3 a carton of milk

4 a packet of biscuits

5 a bag of flour

6 a jar of tomato sauce

THE BiG Quest

Supermarket World

1 Where are we, Ania?

We're in Supermarket World.

2 **Challenge**

Buy the ingredients to make a party meal for you and your friends. You've got 10 minutes. **Win** everything in the **trolley**!

Let's make pizzas and milkshakes. They're my favourites.

3 Why don't we make a healthy party meal?

Good idea! Healthy and delicious! I'm sure we'll win. Let's go!

4 **BEFORE YOU READ** This story is about buying food for a party. What do you think Ania and Ben will buy?

5 Listen, read and check your ideas. 🔊 158

6 **AFTER YOU READ** Watch the story video. ▷ Complete the activities. **AB Page 97**

1 **REMEMBER THE STORY** Read. Say the missing words.

1 How much ▬▬ do we need?

2 How many ▬▬ of tuna do we need?

3 We don't need much ▬▬.

4 We don't need many ▬▬.

5 Let's get a lot of ▬▬.

6 You've got a lot of healthy ▬▬.

2 Find *much*, *many* and *a lot of* in the sentences from the story. Then complete these sentences with the countable nouns or uncountable nouns in the pictures. 📘

1 We can use *a lot of* with …

2 We can use *a lot of* with …

3 We use *How many* to ask about …

4 We use *How much* to ask about …

Look!

We don't use *much* or *many* in affirmative sentences.
~~We've got many bananas.~~ ✘
We've got a lot of bananas. ✔

3 Listen and follow. 🔊 159 **Think** 💭 Imagine you're making a milkshake. Make sentences about the ingredients.

How many	bananas cartons of milk	do we need?
How much	milk ice cream	have we got?

We need	a lot of two	bananas. cartons of milk.
We've got	a lot of	milk. ice cream.
We don't need	a lot of many	bananas. cartons of milk.
We haven't got	a lot of much	milk. ice cream.

4 **Think, pair, share!** Say what you need to make your favourite pizza. Then talk about your partner's pizza.

tuna	cheese	mushrooms	peppers
chicken	jars of tomato sauce		onions

I need two jars of tomato sauce and a lot of onions. I don't need many peppers. I don't need much cheese. I need a lot of tuna.

On his favourite pizza, he's got a lot of tomato sauce and a lot of onions. He hasn't got many peppers. He hasn't got much cheese. He's got a lot of tuna.

Where can we go shopping?

We can buy fruit at the greengrocer's.

Sophie

1 Look. Which of these foods do you eat?

2 Look and read. Which foods have got vitamin C in them? What is vitamin C good for?

sunlight – Our bodies need sunlight to make vitamin D.

Vitamins

Fruit and vegetables are good for us because they've got a lot of vitamins in them. Vitamins are important to keep us healthy. The names of the vitamins are usually letters, but there are eight B vitamins which work together in a group. The B vitamins are called B1, B2, B3, etc. The picture shows you where to find vitamins.

apples C

bananas B6 C

broccoli A C E K

cabbage A B5 B6 C K

carrots A

kiwi fruits C

leeks B6

mangoes A

oranges C

peas B1

peppers A C

potatoes B6 C

spinach A C K

sunflower seeds E

tomatoes A C

eyes C

teeth C D

brain B C

muscles D E

heart E

skin A B C

blood C E

bones C D K

energy B

3 What are these foods good for? Match. Can you add another fruit or vegetable to each sentence?

1 Broccoli, carrots and mangoes are good for
2 Kiwi fruits and oranges help stop coughs and colds
3 Sunflower seeds are good for
4 Cabbage and peas help your body
5 Spinach is good for your

a and they're good for your skin.
b make energy from food.
c your eyes and skin.
d bones.
e your heart.

4 **Think, pair, share!** What vitamins have your favourite fruit and vegetables got in them?

Rosa

Where can we go shopping?

I love going to markets.

1 **BEFORE YOU READ** Look at the photos. Where is this market?

2 **Think** What do you think you can do at this market?

3 Read and listen. 🔊 161 Were your ideas in the leaflet?

All about the market in Santiago de Compostela
Amazing products, friendly stallholders and a lot to see and do!

Santiago de Compostela is the capital of Galicia, in Spain. The market in Santiago is more than 150 years old. Markets have been an important part of life in Galicia for many years. There's a lot to taste, to see, to smell and to hear. Here are some ideas for your shopping basket.

Buy some scallops and take a shell home as a souvenir! The scallop shell is the symbol of the city.

Try some Padrón peppers, but be careful: one or two are always very hot!

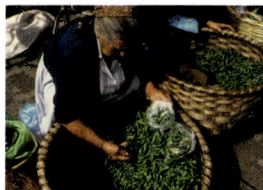

Ask the stallholder for a small piece of cheese to taste. Then buy some to take home.

Stop and look at the beautiful flowers at the florist's. Choose some for your home or for a friend.

You can do other things at the market, too!

Are you hungry? Come to our café! Our chefs use food from the market. We serve all sorts of fish and vegetables, as well as traditional potato omelettes. Have you bought some peppers or scallops in the market? We can cook them for you!

Do you like cooking? We've got courses for everybody. Children can learn to make cakes and biscuits. Adults can learn to cook our wonderful fish. Adventurous cooks can learn to cook with Galician seaweed!

ℹ️ **Useful information**
Opening times: Monday – Saturday, 7 am – 3 pm
Address: Rua de Ameas, Santiago de Compostela

Big Values!
Eat fresh, healthy food and buy it from local farmers.

4 **AFTER YOU READ**
Complete the activities. **AB Page 100**

1 Listen to Rosa talking to her grandma. 🔊 162 **Answer.**

Who did Rosa go to the market with?

| her mum | her brother | her dad | her grandma |

2 Listen again. 🔊 162 **Answer the questions.** 📝

1 Who bought flowers?
2 Whose birthday party is it tomorrow?
3 Who bought some sports shoes?
4 Who went to a cookery class?
5 Who went to a café?
6 Who likes Rosa's biscuits?

3 **Think, pair, share!** What special things can you buy at a market in your area?

4 **Complete the activities.** AB Page 101

Lesson 9 Writing The **Big Write** AB Pages 102–103

Lesson 10 **THE BIG QUESTION REVIEW**

REVIEW VIDEO

1 Watch and answer the questions on the review video. ▶

2 Look back at the unit and say the missing words.
Then compare your answers on the Big Question poster.

Shopping in ☐ shops helps others.

We can buy ☐ at the greengrocer's.

There are a lot of shops on the ☐ Street.

I love going to ☐ .

I like buying my favourite food at the ☐ .

We can use the ☐ to buy a lot of things.

3 **Communicate** 💬 **Ask and answer.**

Which is your favourite answer?

'I love going to markets.' Vegetables from local farmers are delicious!

4 **Complete the self-evaluation activities.** AB Page 103

1 **Complete. Look and write what the people bought.**

| a book | a tennis racket | ~~some bread~~ | some carrots | some shorts |

1 I _____was_____ shopping at the baker's. _I bought some bread._

2 I was _____ at the greengrocer's. _____

3 I _____ at the bookshop. _____

4 _____ at the clothes shop. _____

5 _____ at the sports shop. _____

2 **Read and match the questions and answers.**

1 What were you doing on Saturday morning?

2 Did you win?

3 What were you doing on Saturday afternoon?

4 Did you see a whale?

a Yes, we did. We won 3–2.

b No, I didn't, but I saw a shark.

c I was playing football.

d I was visiting the aquarium.

3 **Answer the questions for you.**

1 What were you doing on Saturday morning? _____

2 What were you doing on Saturday afternoon? _____

3 What were you doing on Saturday evening? _____

4 **Communicate** 💬 **Ask and answer the questions from activity 3.**
Think of _Did you ...?_ questions to ask your partner.

What were you doing on Saturday morning?

I was cycling.

Did you go to the park?

No, I didn't. I went to the forest.

5 Complete with *much*, *many* or *a lot of*.

1 How _____*many*_____ eggs have we got?

We haven't got _____*many*_____ eggs.

2 How _____ bananas have we got?

We haven't got _____ bananas.

3 How _____ juice have we got?

We've got _____ juice.

4 How _____ cheese have we got?

We haven't got _____ cheese.

5 How _____ oranges have we got?

We've got _____ oranges.

6 How _____ cartons of milk have we got?

We haven't got _____ cartons of milk.

6 Think 💭 Look and write sentences.

Shopping list

1 *We need a lot of milk.*

2 _____

3 _____

4 _____

5 _____

6 _____

7 Communicate 💬 Work in pairs. Imagine you're making favourite sandwiches. Say what you need.

We need a lot of bread.

1 BEFORE YOU READ Look at the pictures. In which paragraphs of the text do you think you'll find these words?

> boat   dress   elephant   Europe   fashion   Japan   peace   swan

2 Read and listen. 🔊164 Check your ideas.

3 AFTER YOU READ Ask and answer.

> What interesting things did you discover about origami?

> I discovered that the word *origami* comes from two Japanese words.

4 Complete the activities. **AB Page 104**

What is origami?

1   This boat, this elephant and this swan are origami models. Origami is the art of paper-folding. The word origami comes from two Japanese words: *oru* means **fold** and *kami* means paper.

2   There are a lot of different ways of making origami models, but they all use paper and no scissors or glue. The boat and the elephant are made from one piece of square paper. The piece of paper for the boat was huge — as long as a football pitch! The swan is an example of a different style of origami. The artist made it with a lot of small models.

What is the history of origami?

3   The Chinese invented paper more than 2,000 years ago, and they made simple paper models. Paper arrived in Japan 500 years later, and they started to fold paper, too. At first, paper was very expensive and they only made origami models for special occasions, like weddings. Later, when paper was cheaper, people started to fold paper for fun.

4   People started folding paper in Europe, too. There's a picture of a paper boat in a European book about **astronomy**. The book is more than 500 years old.

In this painting by Auguste Joseph Trupheme, the boy on the right has got some origami animals.

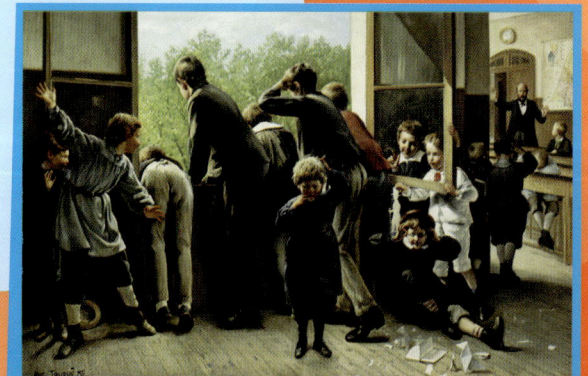

1 **Think** 💭 Read the text again. How many different origami models are mentioned in the text? What are they?

2 **Think, pair, share!** Why do you think origami is popular?

3 **Create** 💡 Follow the instructions and make an origami butterfly. **AB Page 105** ▶

Who does origami now?

5   In the 20th century, Akira Yoshizawa, from Japan, designed more than 50,000 models. He made origami popular and people all over the world started to fold paper. Yoshizawa is called the grandfather of origami.

6   The **crane** is one of the most popular origami models in the world, because of a Japanese tradition. People believe that somebody with 1,000 cranes can **make a wish**. Now groups of people meet and fold cranes to ask for peace, or to help people with problems, or wildlife in danger.

7   Artists, engineers and fashion **designers** all use origami in their work. Obviously, paper dresses and shoes aren't very practical! But some designers fold fabrics to make clothes in the same way as origami models are made. Issey Miyake was one of the first designers to use origami in his designs. His clothes are both fashionable and fun!

A puppet show

1 **Think** 💭 Number the project stages in order in your notebook. 📓 Then look at pages 130–133 and check. WHOLE CLASS

a Present your show to your class.

b Practise your puppet show.

c Make your puppets.

d Find out the characters and stories your group likes.

e Choose a story and characters for your puppet show.

f Think about the stories in *Oxford Thinkers 4*.

Think about it

2 **Think** 💭 Answer the questions. WHOLE CLASS

1 Which game worlds did the children visit in *Oxford Thinkers* 4?

2 Which game world did you like best?

3 Which character is …

    a the bravest?   **b** the funniest?   **c** the cleverest?

4 What do you think of Trick and Lucky?

3 **Communicate** 💬 Look at the pictures and answer. WHOLE CLASS

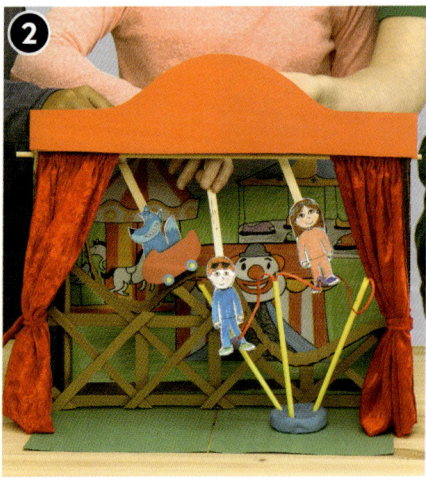

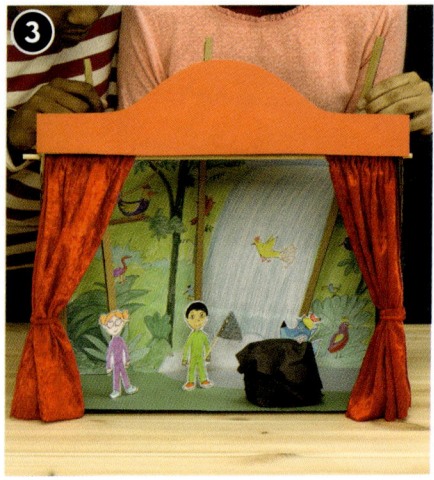

1 Which characters can you see in the photos?

2 Match the photos to the game worlds.

    a Bird World   **b** Winter World   **c** Freddy's Funfair World

3 What props can help to tell the stories? What props can you see in the photos?

4 Find out which story characters your group wants in the puppet show. Make notes in your Activity Book. **AB Page 106 Activity 1** **PROJECT GROUP**

Pupil 1 Which *Oxford Thinkers* girl character do you like best?

Pupil 2 Which *Oxford Thinkers* boy character do you like best?

Pupil 3 Who do you want in the play: Trick, Lucky, or Trick and Lucky?

Pupil 4 Which *Oxford Thinkers* 4 story do you want to choose for your show?

Choose

5 **Collaborate** Tell your group your information. Choose one story for your play. You can change the characters. **PROJECT GROUP**

Three of us like Lily best.

Everybody wants Trick in the play.

Let's do the Fashion World story. It's got Trick in it.

Let's change the characters to Mason and Lily.

6 Listen and follow. 🔊 165 **Then look at the pictures and say.** PROJECT GROUP

Should	we	choose a director? use sound effects? make some simple props? make an advert for our show?	Good idea! Why not? I don't think we need to.

1 **2** **3**

English in use

We use *Should we ... ?* to suggest how to do something better.

7 Create 💡 **Choose jobs. Make your puppets and practise your show.**

AB Page 106 Activities 2–3 PROJECT GROUP

Step 1
Decide who is going to use each puppet and make them.

Step 2
Decide who is going to be the director of the show. Decide who is going to do the sound effects. Decide what props you need and who is going to make or bring them.

Step 3
Practise your show two or three times. The director can give some advice.

DIRECTOR

Step 4
Make an advert for your puppet show.

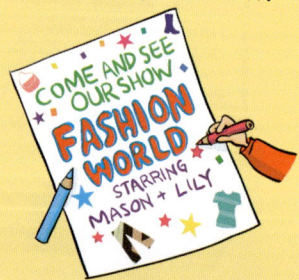

COME AND SEE OUR SHOW
FASHION WORLD
STARRING MASON + LILY

8 Think 💭 Read. Which advice from the director of the puppet show is good?

> You should talk more loudly.

> Remember to make the puppets look at each other.

> You should talk more quickly.

> You shouldn't look over the desk.

9 Present your puppet show to your class. Then answer questions from your class. WHOLE CLASS

> Welcome to our puppet show.

> We're going to do the Fashion World story.

> Why did you decide to do this story?

> The main characters are Lily and Mason. They're our favourites. Trick is in the story, too.

Come and See our show Fashion World starring Mason and Lily

10 Think 💭 Think about the project and answer the questions. WHOLE CLASS

1 What did you enjoy about this project?
2 Which puppet show do you think was the best? Why?

International Day of Peace

1 Read and listen. 🔊 166 What do people do on the International Day of Peace?

The International Day of Peace is on 21ˢᵗ September each year. On this day, countries should stop fighting and everybody should think about making peace. Many people wear a dove, the symbol of peace, on 21ˢᵗ September. In the United Nations, they ring a special bell every year. Children collected coins from 60 different countries. The United Nations' bell is made from these coins.

2 Listen, point and say. 🔊 167

1 dove   **2** heart   **3** bell   **4** handprint   **5** peace symbol

3 Read and match to the Day of Peace artwork. 📘

1 This illustrates the Day of Peace because the children are co-operating to make a star.

3 This illustrates the Day of Peace because the two hands make a heart. A heart is the symbol of love, not fighting.

2 These people from different countries are standing together to make a dove. The dove is the international symbol of peace.

4 This heart is made from children's handprints. The children have worked together to make a picture.

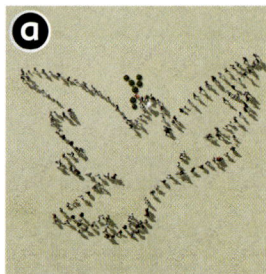 
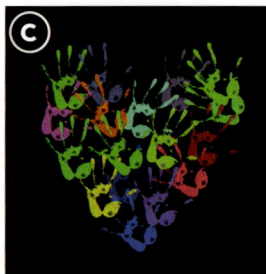 

4 Think, pair, share! Answer the questions.

1 Why is the United Nations' bell a symbol of peace?

2 Can you describe a peaceful scene? What can you see? What can you hear?

3 What can you do for peace in your school?

Pancake Day

1 Read and listen. 🔊 169 When is Pancake Day?

Pancake Day is a special day in many countries. In France, it's called *Mardi Gras* or *Fat Tuesday*. The date changes every year, but it's always in February or March. People make and eat a lot of **pancakes** on Pancake Day. In some places there are pancake races. People run through the streets with a **frying pan** and a pancake. They have to **toss** the pancake and run at the same time!

2 Listen, point and say. 🔊 170

1 pancake
2 frying pan
3 toss

3 Read and match the pictures to the recipe. Then listen and check. 🔊 171

1 one spoonful of vegetable oil / 300 ml milk / 100 g flour / two eggs

2

3

4

5 01:00

6

a Add a spoonful of the pancake batter to a hot frying pan.

b Put the flour in a bowl. Add the eggs and about 50 ml of milk.

c Eat your pancake with lemon, sugar, chocolate sauce or ice cream.

d You need flour, eggs, oil and milk.

e Cook for a minute. Toss your pancake. Cook the other side.

f Start mixing. Slowly add the rest of the milk and the oil. Mix well to make your pancake batter.

4 **Think, pair, share!** When do you eat pancakes? What do you like to eat with them?

ACKNOWLEDGEMENTS

Back cover photograph: Oxford University Press building/
David Fisher

Main illustrations by: John Haslam.

Other illustrations by: Akbar Ali/The Organisation pp.9 (Native
Americans), 16 (Native Americans), 46-47, 63, 70; Ilias Arahovitis/
Beehive Illustration p.86; Judy Brown pp.27, 45 (Glossary),
48-49, 57 (Glossary), 75, 81, 88, 90, 132, 135; Laura Catalan/Good
Illustration pp.18, 19, 30, 31, 42, 43, 60, 61, 72, 73, 84, 85, 102,
103, 115, 126-127; Anna Hancock/Beehive Illustration pp.4 (b, d),
5 (Ex5), 8, 10, 16 (Big Values), 20, 22, 28 (Big Values), 32, 34 (Ex4),
40 (Big Values), 50, 52, 58 (Big Values), 62, 64, 70 (Big Values), 74,
76, 82 (Big Values), 92, 94, 100, 104, 106, 108, 112 (Big Values),
116, 118, 124; Javier Joaquin/The Organisation pp.41, 134; Kelly
Kennedy/Sylve Poggio Artist's Agency pp.4 (e), 11, 14, 23, 26,
35, 38, 53, 56, 65, 68, 77, 80, 89, 95, 98, 107, 110, 114, 119, 122;
Angeles Peinador/Beehive Illustration pp.28 (Ex3), 34 (Ex3), 93,
99, 117, 123; Mark Ruffle (all classroom backgrounds); Sally
Wern Comport pp.44-45.

Commissioned photography by: Graham Alder/MM Studios pp.21,
27, 50, 47, 49, 89, 91, 130, 131, 133; Gareth Boden pp.116;
Vanessa Marshall pp.8, 11, 17.

*The Publishers would like to thank the following for their kind permission
to reproduce photographs and other copyright material*: Alamy:
pp.4 (computer game/Anatolii Babii), (Sophie/Geoff du Feu),
5 (Sophie/Geoff du Feu), 10 (2/Richard Wayman), (3/Sinibomb
Images), (6/Bart Pro), (7/Juice Images), (9/Directphoto Collection),
(10/Mint Images Limited), 12 (4/Jessie Jane Smith/Stockimo),
15 (Monarch butterfly Danaus plexippus Egg/Don Johnston_IH),
20 (Male Amur leopard/cgwp.co.uk), 21 (rhino/dpa picture
alliance archive), 24 (1/Joe Blossom), (2/Olaf Doering), (3/Jochen
Tack), (4/Piero Cruciatti), (5/blickwinkel), (6/Julie Fryer Images),
28 (rhino/dpa picture alliance archive), 35 (girl hiding/Martin
Williams), 50 (Junior/Tetra Images), (Sophie/Geoff du Feu),
52 (1/Gareth McCormack), (8/joan gravell), (9/NASA Archive),
(Sophie/Geoff du Feu), 53 (Junior/Tetra Images), (Sophie/Geoff du
Feu), 57 (Giovanni Domenico Cassini/Science History Images),
59 (Junior/Tetra Images), (Sophie/Geoff du Feu), 63 (Divit/
dbimages), (Sophie/Geoff du Feu), 64 (3/Blend Images), (5/Peter
Titmuss), (6/jacky chapman), 65 (heart cake/Image Source), 66 (4/
blickwinkel), 69 (Sophie/Geoff du Feu), 70 (Divit/dbimages),
71 (Divit/dbimages), (Sophie/Geoff du Feu), 74 (Amelia/Orange
Stock Photo Production Inc.), (bumper cars/David Bagnall),
75 (rubber boat/Sebastijan Polak), 76 (3/Bruce Leighty - Sports
Images), (4/Elly Godfroy), (5/Marc Romanelli/Blend Images), (10/
Qrt), 77 (Amelia/Orange Stock Photo Production Inc.), 78 (3/
David Bagnall), (4/Elliot Nichol), (5/Family - People), 82 (rubber
boat/Sebastijan Polak), 83 (Amelia/Orange Stock Photo Production
Inc.), 96 (1/Radius Images), 101 (Sophie/Geoff du
Feu), 104 (Sophie/Geoff du Feu), 105 (picking coffee bean berries/
ton koene), 106 (1/Mark Waugh), (2/Ian Dagnall), (7/Justin Kase
z12z), (8/Jeffrey Blackler), (10/Kumar Sriskandan), 108 (Sophie/
Geoff du Feu), 111 (2/ton koene), (3/ton koene), (5/Jake Lyell),
(6/WorldFoto), (8/Richard Human), 112 (family working/Peter
Horree), 113 (Sophie/Geoff du Feu), 117 (market/Kevin George),
(Sophie/Geoff du Feu), 118 (6/Fotomatador), (10/Ian G Dagnall),
120 (4/studiomode), 123 (Sophie/Geoff du Feu), 124 (cheese on
display/Lucas Vallecillos), (market/Kevin George), (scallops/Juan
Bautista), (women selling pimentos pimientos/David A. Barnes),
125 (shoe market/Lightworks Media), (Sophie/Geoff du Feu),
135 (school pancake race/Scott Bairstow);

Bridgeman Images: pp.57 (Galileo/Galileo, English School, (20th
century)/Private Collection/© Look and Learn), 128 (The Class
Pranksters. Auguste Joseph Trupheme/The Class Pranksters,
(oil on canvas), Trupheme, Auguste Joseph (1836-98)/Private
Collection/Photo © Christie's Images); DK Images: p.81 (Lava
lamp in plastic bottle/Howard Shooter); Getty: pp.4 (Ben/
Tatyana Aleksieva Photography/Moment), (Yurta/VisitBritain/
Joanna Henderson), 5 (Ben/Tatyana Aleksieva Photography/
Moment), (Tadi/Camille Tokerud Photography Inc./The Image Bank),
9 (butterfly/StevenRussellSmithPhotos), 10 (Ania/Alexander
Trinitatov), 11 (Ania/Alexander Trinitatov), 12 (1/Guas), (2/
Bull's-Eye Arts), (3/rtbilder), (6/Maxal Tamor), 15 (Monarch
Butterfly/StevenRussellSmithPhotos), (Monarch Caterpillar
eating Milkweed/Elliotte Rusty Harold), (Monarch Caterpillar
in cocoon/Jacob Hamblin), 17 (Ania/Alexander Trinitatov),
(Tess/Judy Kennamer), 20 (aligator/Arto Hakola), 22 (1/Veronika
Synenko), (2/Attila JANDI), (3/ChaiyonS021), (4/konmesa), (5/
ZRyzner), (6/meunierd), (7/leungchopan), (8/leungchopan), (9/
Arto Hakola), (10/Dale Mitchell), 27 (gray tree frog/IrinaK),
29 (Ania/Alexander Trinitatov), 32 (gloves/Boris Sosnovyy), (Nico/
Hurst Photo), (scarf/mimo), (Tess/Judy Kennamer), (wellies/
SP-Photo), 33 (Ania/Alexander Trinitatov), (Ethan/sanneberg),
35 (Nico/Hurst Photo), 36 (1/nito), (2/koll), (3/Shevel Artur), (4/
SP-Photo), (5/mimo), (6/Boris Sosnovyy), (Tess/Judy Kennamer),
39 (Ania/Alexander Trinitatov), 40 (BBQ/nd3000), (Ethan/
sanneberg), (July 4th cake/Arina P Habich), 41 (Ania/Alexander
Trinitatov), (Ethan/sanneberg), (Nico/Hurst Photo), (Tess/
Judy Kennamer), 50 (peacock/e X p o s e), 51 (Ania/Alexander
Trinitatov), 52 (4/salajean), (5/armmphoto), (6/George Martinus),
(7/Byelikova Oksana), 54 (1/Ratikova), (3/Ondrej Prosicky), (4/e
X p o s e), (5/Alison Roosenberg), (6/Carmine Arienzo), 57 (Ania/
Alexander Trinitatov), (Unmanned spacecraft/3000ad), 59 (Angel
falls/LysFoto), (Ania/Alexander Trinitatov), 62 (washing car/
gorillaimages), 64 (8/PAKULA PIOTR), (9/TinnaPong), 66 (1/Ami
Parikh), (2/BestPhotoPlus), (3/vvoe), (5/gorillaimages), 71 (Thai
style food carriers/natkom), 74 (Tess/Judy Kennamer), 75 (Alenka/
Oleg_Mit), 76 (2/Sergey Lavrentev), (6/Pavel L Photo and Video),
(7/Skully), 77 (Tess/Judy Kennamer),
78 (1/a_v_d), (2/Bertl123), 82 (Alenka/Oleg_Mit), (Alenka/
Oleg_Mit), (Tess/Judy Kennamer), 92 (Charlie/Syda Productions),
(London buses/William Perugini), (Tess/Judy Kennamer),
93 (Okan/istanbul_image_video), 95 (Charlie/Syda Productions),
(ill boy/Syda Productions), 96 (5/ESB Professional), (6/zhu difeng),
(Tess/Judy Kennamer), 100 (Okan/istanbul_image_video), (yellow
submarine/Teguh Mujiono), 101 (Charlie/Syda Productions),
(drawing/Africa Studio), (Okan/istanbul_image_video), (Tess/
Judy Kennamer), 104 (laptop garden/Alex Brylov), 105 (Fabio/
Tracy Whiteside), (Tess/Judy Kennamer), 106 (3/06photo), (6/
emei), (7/Capricorn Studio), 111 (1/James Jones Jr), (4/Pecold),
(9/sylv1rob1), (10/tsyhun), (Tess/Judy Kennamer), 112 (Fabio/
Tracy Whiteside), 113 (Fabio/Tracy Whiteside), (Tess/Judy
Kennamer), 116 (Ania/Alexander Trinitatov), 117 (Rosa/Gelpi),
118 (1/Tobik), (2/mangostock), (3/Dima Sidelnikov), (4/Oscar
Johns), (7/ElenaK78), 119 (high street UK/IR Stone), 120 (2/Asier
Romero), (5/M. Unal Ozmen), (6/Svetlana Foote), (Ania/Alexander
Trinitatov), 123 (cabbage/Palokha Tetiana), (carrots/Lotus
Images), (kiwis/Roman Samokhin), (leeks/Edward Westmacott),
(mangoes/Maks Narodenko), (oranges/Luiscar74), (peas/
v.s.anandhakrishna), (peppers/Nattika), (red apples/Natalia7),
(sun in sky/Vibrant Image Studio), (sunflower seeds/ninoninos),
124 (Rosa/Gelpi), (street flower shop/Elnur), 125 (Ania/Alexander
Trinitatov), (Rosa/Gelpi), 128 (paper elephant/Dado Photos),
(paper swan/Tiger Images), (paper cranes/Jules_Kitano),
(woman in paper dresss/Kiselev Andrey Valerevich), 134 (b/
ANURAK PONGPATIMET), (c/viviamo), (d/paulaphoto).

76 (8/craftvision/E+), 83 (Noah/keeweeboy), 92 (Rubik's Cube/
fzant), 93 (Lily/studio157), 96 (3/antfoto), 99 (Lily/studio157),
101 (Lily/studio157), 104 (Noah/keeweeboy), (Poppy/dcdebs),
106 (5/kodachrome25), (Noah/keeweeboy), 107 (Noah/
keeweeboy), (Poppy/dcdebs), 113 (Dev/Instants), (ice cream/
TheLionRoar), (Noah/keeweeboy), (Poppy/dcdebs), 116 (Dev/
Instants), (Eve/kali9), 118 (Dev/Instants), 119 (Dev/Instants),
(Eve/kali9), 120 (3/craftvision), 125 (Dev/Instants), (Eve/kali9),
(Lily/studio157); Mary Evans Picture Library: p.58 (Mary
Evans Picture Library); Nature Picture Library: p.29 (Montserrat
mountain chicken frog/Roland Seitre); Oxford University Press:
pp.4 (Mason/Shelly Perry/Getty Images), 8 (Mason/Shelly Perry/
Getty Images), 10 (8/Mike Stone), 12 (Mason/Shelly Perry/Getty
Images), 17 (Mason/Shelly Perry/Getty Images), 32 (Mason/
Shelly Perry/Getty Images), 34 (Mason/Shelly Perry/Getty
Images), 35 (Mason/Shelly Perry/Getty Images), 41 (Mason/Shelly
Perry/Getty Images), 44 (Black Beauty by Anna Sewell/Oxford
University Press), 50 (Cape town/michealjung/Shutterstock),
52 (10/Rich Carey/Shutterstock), 54 (2/Corbis/Digital Stock),
59 (Mason/Shelly Perry/Getty Images), 64 (Ryan McVay/
Digital Vision), 75 (Mason/Shelly Perry/Getty Images), 76 (1/
David Madison/Corbis), 81 (Mason/Shelly Perry/Getty Images),
83 (Mason/Shelly Perry/Getty Images), 96 (2/Getty/Barry Austin),
105 (Ice Cream display/Lourens Smak), 106 (4/Chris Hammond),
112 (Ice Cream display/Lourens Smak), 118 (9/Polina Shestakova/
Shutterstock), 120 (1/Martin Wierink/Alamy), 123 (bananas/Maks
Narodenko/Shutterstock), (broccoli/zcw/Shutterstock), (potatoes/
Deep OV/Shutterstock), (spinach/Getty/Thinkstock), (tomatoes/
Lusoimages - Food); PA Images: pp.82 (cave/Robert Anic/PIXSELL),
83 (cave/Robert Anic/PIXSELL); REX: pp.33 (Jurassic Park 1993
still/Amblin/Universal), 39 (scene 1/Amblin/Universal), (scene
2/Amblin/Universal), (scene 3/Amblin/Universal); Science
Photo Library: pp.51 (Saturn/DETLEV VAN RAVENSWAAY),
57 (Saturn/DETLEV VAN RAVENSWAAY), (Voyager spacecraft/
NASA); Shutterstock: pp.4 (Ania/Alexander Trinitatov), (Tess/
Judy Kennamer), (Yellow plastic ducks/J. Long), 5 (Ania/
Alexander Trinitatov), (Tess/Judy Kennamer), 8 (Ania/Alexander
Trinitatov), (autumn leaves/javarman), (snowman/rtbilder),
9 (butterfly/StevenRussellSmithPhotos), 10 (Ania/Alexander
Trinitatov), 11 (Ania/Alexander Trinitatov), 12 (1/Guas), (2/
Bull's-Eye Arts), (3/rtbilder), (6/Maxal Tamor), 15 (Monarch
Butterfly/StevenRussellSmithPhotos), (Monarch Caterpillar
eating Milkweed/Elliotte Rusty Harold), (Monarch Caterpillar
in cocoon/Jacob Hamblin), 17 (Ania/Alexander Trinitatov),
(Tess/Judy Kennamer), 22 (aligator/Arto Hakola), 22 (1/Veronika
Synenko), (2/Attila JANDI), (3/ChaiyonS021), (4/konmesa), (5/
ZRyzner), (6/meunierd), (7/leungchopan), (8/leungchopan), (9/
Arto Hakola), (10/Dale Mitchell), 27 (gray tree frog/IrinaK),
29 (Ania/Alexander Trinitatov), 32 (gloves/Boris Sosnovyy), (Nico/
Hurst Photo), (scarf/mimo), (Tess/Judy Kennamer), (wellies/
SP-Photo), 33 (Ania/Alexander Trinitatov), (Ethan/sanneberg),
35 (Nico/Hurst Photo), 36 (1/nito), (2/koll), (3/Shevel Artur), (4/
SP-Photo), (5/mimo), (6/Boris Sosnovyy), (Tess/Judy Kennamer),
39 (Ania/Alexander Trinitatov), 40 (BBQ/nd3000), (Ethan/
sanneberg), (July 4th cake/Arina P Habich), 41 (Ania/Alexander
Trinitatov), (Ethan/sanneberg), (Nico/Hurst Photo), (Tess/
Judy Kennamer), 50 (peacock/e X p o s e), 51 (Ania/Alexander
Trinitatov), 52 (4/salajean), (5/armmphoto), (6/George Martinus),
(7/Byelikova Oksana), 54 (1/Ratikova), (3/Ondrej Prosicky), (4/e
X p o s e), (5/Alison Roosenberg), (6/Carmine Arienzo), 57 (Ania/
Alexander Trinitatov), (Unmanned spacecraft/3000ad), 59 (Angel
falls/LysFoto), (Ania/Alexander Trinitatov), 62 (washing car/
gorillaimages), 64 (8/PAKULA PIOTR), (9/TinnaPong), 66 (1/Ami
Parikh), (2/BestPhotoPlus), (3/vvoe), (5/gorillaimages), 71 (Thai
style food carriers/natkom), 74 (Tess/Judy Kennamer), 75 (Alenka/
Oleg_Mit), 76 (2/Sergey Lavrentev), (6/Pavel L Photo and Video),
(7/Skully), 77 (Tess/Judy Kennamer),
78 (1/a_v_d), (2/Bertl123), 82 (Alenka/Oleg_Mit), (Alenka/
Oleg_Mit), (Tess/Judy Kennamer), 92 (Charlie/Syda Productions),
(London buses/William Perugini), (Tess/Judy Kennamer),
93 (Okan/istanbul_image_video), 95 (Charlie/Syda Productions),
(ill boy/Syda Productions), 96 (5/ESB Professional), (6/zhu difeng),
(Tess/Judy Kennamer), 100 (Okan/istanbul_image_video), (yellow
submarine/Teguh Mujiono), 101 (Charlie/Syda Productions),
(drawing/Africa Studio), (Okan/istanbul_image_video), (Tess/
Judy Kennamer), 104 (laptop garden/Alex Brylov), 105 (Fabio/
Tracy Whiteside), (Tess/Judy Kennamer), 106 (3/06photo), (6/
emei), (7/Capricorn Studio), 111 (1/James Jones Jr), (4/Pecold),
(9/sylv1rob1), (10/tsyhun), (Tess/Judy Kennamer), 112 (Fabio/
Tracy Whiteside), 113 (Fabio/Tracy Whiteside), (Tess/Judy
Kennamer), 116 (Ania/Alexander Trinitatov), 117 (Rosa/Gelpi),
118 (1/Tobik), (2/mangostock), (3/Dima Sidelnikov), (4/Oscar
Johns), (7/ElenaK78), 119 (high street UK/IR Stone), 120 (2/Asier
Romero), (5/M. Unal Ozmen), (6/Svetlana Foote), (Ania/Alexander
Trinitatov), 123 (cabbage/Palokha Tetiana), (carrots/Lotus
Images), (kiwis/Roman Samokhin), (leeks/Edward Westmacott),
(mangoes/Maks Narodenko), (oranges/Luiscar74), (peas/
v.s.anandhakrishna), (peppers/Nattika), (red apples/Natalia7),
(sun in sky/Vibrant Image Studio), (sunflower seeds/ninoninos),
124 (Rosa/Gelpi), (street flower shop/Elnur), 125 (Ania/Alexander
Trinitatov), (Rosa/Gelpi), 128 (paper elephant/Dado Photos),
(paper swan/Tiger Images), (paper cranes/Jules_Kitano),
(woman in paper dresss/Kiselev Andrey Valerevich), 134 (b/
ANURAK PONGPATIMET), (c/viviamo), (d/paulaphoto).

iStock: pp.4 (Dev/Instants), (Lily/studio157), (Noah/keeweeboy),
5 (Dev/Instants), (Noah/keeweeboy), 10 (4/JenCon), 15 (Monarch
flying/Liliboas), 20 (Dev/Instants), (Lily/studio157), 21 (Noah/
keeweeboy), 22 (Dev/Instants), 23 (Dev/Instants), 24 (Lily/
studio157), 27 (Noah/keeweeboy), 29 (Dev/Instants), (Lily/
studio157), (Noah/keeweeboy), 50 (Dev/Instants), 51 (Camila/
monkeybussinessimages), 54 (Dev/Instants), 58 (Camila/
monkeybussinessimages), 59 (Camila/monkeybussinessimages),
(Dev/Instants), 62 (Lily/studio157), (Noah/keeweeboy), 64 (4/
manfredxy), (10/woolzian), (Lily/studio157), 65 (Lily/studio157),
66 (Noah/keeweeboy), 71 (Lily/studio157), (Noah/keeweeboy),